marooned on Mogmog

marooned on Mogmog

A remote island, a shipwrecked Aussie family, a clash of cultures

JENNIFER BARRIE

HarperCollins*Publishers*

HarperCollins*Publishers*

First published in Australia in 2011
by HarperCollins*Publishers* Australia Pty Limited
ABN 36 009 913 517
harpercollins.com.au

HarperCollins*Publishers*
Level 13, 201 Elizabeth Street, Sydney NSW 2000, Australia
31 View Road, Glenfield, Auckland 0627, New Zealand
A 53, Sector 57, Noida, UP, India
77–85 Fulham Palace Road, London, W6 8JB, United Kingdom
2 Bloor Street East, 20th floor, Toronto, Ontario M4W 1A8, Canada
10 East 53rd Street, New York NY 10022, USA

National Library of Australia Cataloguing-in-Publication entry

Barrie, Jennifer.
   Marooned on Mogmog : a remote island, a shipwrecked Aussie
   family, a clash of cultures / Jennifer Barrie.
   ISBN: 978 0 7322 9243 0 (pbk.)
   Shipwreck victims – Micronesia – Ulithi.
   Voyages and travels.
   Ulithi (Micronesia)--Social life and customs.
910.91647

Cover design by Mark Thacker and Pricilla Nielsen
Cover image island © Henry Wasserman/www.HenryWasserman.com
   All other images supplied by the author
Typeset in 11.5/18pt Adobe Caslon by Kirby Jones
Printed and bound in Australia by Griffin Press
70gsm Classic used by HarperCollins*Publishers* is a natural, recyclable product made
from wood grown in sustainable forests. The manufacturing processes conform to the
environmental regulations in the country of origin, Finland.

5 4 3 2 1   11 12 13 14

Dedicated to Andrew, Diana and Shannon.
If you ever get shipwrecked, you want it to be with these guys.
And to Juanito, chief of all outer islands of Yap State,
a good man with an impossible task.

CONTENTS

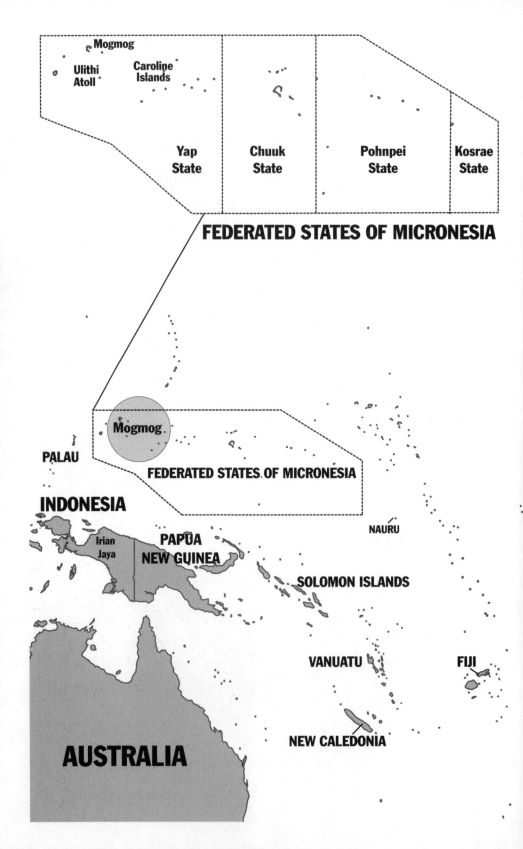

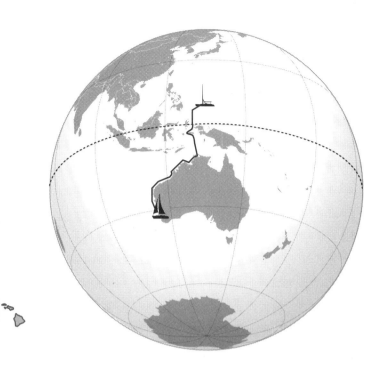

PACIFIC OCEAN

HAWAII

PROLOGUE

Our sea voyage of a lifetime: it started with a dream and felt like it ended with the shipwreck. Ten years of planning, dreaming, plotting and scheming, all gone in one night.

Who's even heard of shipwrecks these days? Hello, this is the 21st century not the 1800s! But that's exactly what happened to us, a modern, mostly normal family from Western Australia. That's how we ended up living on an island in Micronesia that we'd never even heard of before and which, according to the Lonely Planet guide, is home to some of the world's most remote people.

For the previous year my husband, Andrew, and our two daughters — Diana, aged 11, and Shannon, aged nine — and I had been living our dream, sailing our beloved 42-foot catamaran, *Windrider*, around the Pacific. We had planned to keep doing that for at least another year. But the morning after that 12-hour battle with the weather gods, *Windrider* was seated indecorously on the coral beach of this tiny island named Mogmog, with her entire starboard hull ripped out, rudders bent through 90ish degrees, engines out, and communications systems largely rendered useless.

Things looked bad for us; we had chosen not to insure *Windie*. This was for a few reasons. Our normal insurer wouldn't cover us for overseas. When insuring boats for out of Australian waters, all the companies I spoke to required the boat to be surveyed, and that could only be done in Sydney. As we were in Perth, that really wasn't feasible. Even if we had gone to all that trouble, no insurer would have trekked an assessor to Mogmog to look at the thing. So write-off would have been the only solution, and then we would be left with starting from scratch. Having spent eight years getting *Windie*'s systems exactly as we wanted, the thought of starting again with a new boat didn't appeal. It had been a conscious decision to forego the insurance, and it was a decision we would make again, even with hindsight.

We sat on the beach looking at *Windie*, expecting tears that didn't come. Was this the end? Could something be salvaged? Were we unrealistic to even have these thoughts? We didn't know it then, but the very fact that these thoughts were running through our minds meant that we had acknowledged a sliver of a possibility — or maybe an impossibility.

Andrew has a saying: it is possible to eat an elephant as long as you do it one bite at a time. So we set about devouring our elephant, hoping we weren't going to get stomped on.

ONE

CATCHING THE BUG

The seeds of our adventure were sown years ago — on an island, in a tent, with eight-month-old Diana in a portacot hugging a coconut. The island was Direction Island, one of the Cocos Keeling Islands, 900 nautical miles off Western Australia. Our great mate Scott had been telling us about Cocos for years, as his sister was a teacher there at the time, and he had visited quite a bit. He suggested camping on DI, as Direction Island is referred to, and we thought it sounded great.

When I rang Dieter, the ranger, and asked if we were able to camp on DI, he came back with, 'Why do you want to do *that*?' his voice full of incredulity.

'Um, coz it might be fun?'

'Well, you can camp wherever you bloody-well like, but I think you're nuts!'

So with his blessing of sorts, we packed up Diana; Andrew's mum, Dawn; and all our camping gear and flew to Cocos.

We spent the first week in a wooden chalet and had an amazing time, meeting the locals, going to the cyclone shelter that doubles as a bar, playing golf. The first four holes go up one side of the airstrip, and then you all stop and watch the plane land then continue down the other side. There are fully stocked Eskies at every hole.

Next we set off for DI. In days gone by, this island was used for the copra trade, so a coconut palm plantation covers the land area. We set up camp under a palm tree with our two tents and a portacot for Diana.

A word about Diana: she had finally come along after six years of trying, two heartbreaking miscarriages and many IVF attempts. She is a miracle. The emotional rollercoaster that is IVF had been really taking its toll — we had been at the end of our ropes. Simon, my obstetrician, realised this and sat with us for over an hour, saying that in spite of our failures thus far he truly believed that IVF would work for us. He's not a bedside manner sort of guy, so we decided on one more try. The result was Diana, who on DI was sitting bald-headed and very blue-eyed, peering out from underneath the brim of a large knitted hat, with a huge knitted rose on the front. Shannon, in contrast, was conceived with little more than a twinkle in her daddy's eye, 10 months later.

The beach on DI is pristine white; the ocean is crystal clear; and at one end there is a rip snorkel: a narrow, long channel of water where the current flies through so fast that there is absolutely no chance of swimming against it. You scramble down the rocks with your snorkel gear, throw yourself into the water and swim as hard as you can against the current. That way you get a chance to see the sharks, coral, wrasse and myriad other fish as you fly by. Then it spits you out at the other end and you stagger back up the rocks and do it all again.

On the island, there is an undercover area with tables and chairs. It is filled with years of memorabilia left by international yachties who stay and rest in the anchorage as they make their way across the Indian Ocean to either South Africa or the Mediterranean. There are thousands of flags, wood carvings, bottles with messages and pieces of artwork. It would take a full week to look at everything there.

While on DI we met a bunch of these yachties. There was German South African Joe, who travelled the world fixing unfixable telephones; Ross and Sue from Dampier; Gail and Steve; Paul and Linda; and and and and …

Our week was full of hilarious incidents and gave us a peek into a world we had no idea existed, the world of globetrotting yachties. What immediately appealed to us was that all these people of all ages and from all walks of life had decided to largely give up on the rat race. Gone were the deadlines and timeframes. Gone were the day-to-day stresses of normal life. These people would wake up in the morning and talk about where they might like to go next … or not. It was completely up to them. The freedom inherent in this lifestyle was something we could not get out of our heads.

One night was Paul's birthday, so there was a surprise party for him in the undercover area. It was a raucous night, with crazy Brazilians leading the way, drinking way too much whatever it was. In the course of the evening, Andrew asked Paul if he had received his 'real' birthday present from Linda yet. No, came the reply, sadly he had not. He said that if he did, he would flash the mastlight. Later on, after the yachties all dribbed and drabbed back to their boats, Paul's mastlight started flashing. Ha! Within 15 minutes, every mastlight in the vicinity was flashing! You could hear the laughter all around the bay.

This was a lifestyle we had to pursue, sooner or later.

I have always had an affinity with water. As a kid, I grew up near the Swan River in Perth, and my friends and I spent the afternoons after school catching tadpoles in the swamps or fossicking in the water. Water has always been associated with calmness for me. Later, when I needed to deal with teenage angst, I would always head to the river to calm down and think.

Andrew grew up canoeing on the river with his dad; I grew up with sailing dinghies. When Andrew and I teamed up as teenagers, we spent a lot of time paddling and sailing on the river for fun. It was a way to get off and be by ourselves, more than anything else.

* * *

After that DI trip, it was only ever going to be a question of when we would organise our own time out of the rat race. Meanwhile years went by, and life in the Barrie household was chaotic and happy. Andrew and I had long ago sat down and worked out what we wanted from a home life, and the result was a house full of kids: ours; friends'; the neighbours'; the girls' classmates from the school directly over the road, plus their parents; and our beloved old dog, Molly.

Our street is small, and most households have kids at the school, too, so over time there has come to be a strong sense of friendship and community, more as you would've found in the 1960s than what you might expect today.

We also have a large and close network of friends, and I've come to realise just how great these people are, and how fortunate we are to have them. They are not the sort of people who express sorrow at a situation and offer condolences; rather, they get moving and help solve problems. Our front door was only closed when we were asleep, and everyone felt free to wander in and out for a chat or drink, to organise who was getting which kids from where, maybe to have a meal, watch the footie or sit in the spa out the back.

All of this was woven around a frenetic work life. Andrew and I both ran our own independent businesses from home — he was a carpenter doing home renovations around our area, while I ran a dictaphone business and taught flute at a number of Perth schools. There was frequent backstopping for each other and sharing the kid duties. I would liaise for Andrew with his clients, and he would do deliveries for mine, and one of us would be home for the end of school.

To leave all this behind would be a huge undertaking: to commit to ending both businesses, resigning from the Education Department, painting the house, moving from it and renting it out. Once we had taken these steps, there would be no turning back.

Timing-wise, it seemed that the perfect time would be when the girls were eight and nine. In a few years, they wouldn't want to be anywhere near us. Also, given our ages, Andrew and I wanted to do this while we could. You never know what's around the corner. Andrew's dad passed away suddenly at 53. Andrew always has in the back of his mind that this could be his position as well.

The girls' education was a concern, but when I talked to their teachers, I was told about the School of Isolated and Distance Education (SIDE), a school for kids all around the world who can't get to a normal school. The results coming from SIDE are generally better than for most other schools, and the resources are excellent. Next we went for a visit and met the staff. It was impressive. Enrolling Diana and Shannon in SIDE meant that I wasn't going to be home schooling, and that someone with way more knowledge than me was responsible for curriculum.

So we decided to give it a go — for two years, so that Diana could get back to finish primary school with her classmates, who are a seriously great bunch of kids.

* * *

When we announced our plans, friends were fully supportive. Our parents were not. That was no surprise. Both Andrew's parents and mine were convinced we had been trying to kill their granddaughters from the time they were born. They were suspicious of us going sailing, putting the girls within spitting distance of stingrays or man-eating sharks. My flying lessons and scuba diving didn't impress them. And as for the .308 rifle club lessons that Andrew and I took Diana and Shannon to every Saturday afternoon, well that was hardly the behaviour of responsible parents, either. But we have always said that life should be lived, and our kids have been brought up on this philosophy. And so far they are happy, capable and responsible small people who look for the fun in life.

Now we were going to up the ante. To our parents' minds, living on a boat meant nothing but endless possibilities for placing all four of us in mortal danger: cyclones, man overboard (MOB), sharks, crocs, pirates.

It was a drag putting up with the criticism, but there was an 'upside' for me. Practically the only time my parents talked to each other in 25 years was when they were agreeing on how stupid we were! That had to be worth something. Very quietly, little bit by little bit, they pointed out the hazards and we batted away each objection until it became clear we were going regardless. And then out it came: what they really thought. But there was no deterring us, and they knew that.

TWO

WINDRIDER

Maybe half the reason we couldn't convince our parents our trip was a good idea was the state of our boat, *Windrider*. She was a real 'renovator's delight'.

Our previous boat was a 19-foot Douglascraft v-berth cabin cruiser, manufactured in 1968. We had had it for years before the girls came along, and we were determined that we were not going to let a little thing like parenthood get in the way of our lifestyle. Diana had her first trip to Rottnest, the party island just off the coast near Perth, the day we took her home from hospital, aged four days.

There are only 19 months between Diana and Shan. When they were little, we would pack the boat to stuffing point with portacot, high chair, two kids' bags, our own baggage, Eskies, food, bottles, nappies, beer, toys, wine — you get the picture —

and off we'd go in the 19-foot boat for a week at a time to our beloved Rotto.

We'd pull up to the pub jetty, which was the party jetty on the party island, and we all had a ball. The kids could swim before they could walk. Everyone knew them and looked out for them. It was fantastic. At first they slept in the portacot out the back, with a tarpaulin draped over to keep the rain or sun out, and we slept in the v-berth. Then they grew, and grew … and grew; soon the portacot was out, and we were all in the v-berth together, which worked for about a month. Then they started pushing and kicking in their sleep, and Andrew and I gave up and went to sleep on the back under the tarp.

One night, I woke up and could feel that my feet were wet. I pulled them up and went back to sleep. Then I realised that my feet were wet again, so I pulled them up some more and settled back down to sleep. Soon I was a ball with nowhere to go. I opened one eye, and Andrew had curled up into a corresponding ball next to me. Then I looked down to see water filling the transom area and up the deck to where our feet had been originally. Shit! The stern was now sitting on the bottom which, fortunately, was not far away! Time for a new boat!

The search started at home in Western Australia then extended via the internet into the Eastern States as well. At first the hunt was for monos, which is boatie speak for single-hulled vessels. Hundreds of hours later we'd looked at them on screens, in magazines and newspapers and in the flesh. We'd been to boat shows until we were blue in the face. And even though we had a reasonable budget and thought we knew what we wanted, nothing seemed quite right. Always in the backs of our minds was the dream of some day going cruising.

After about eight months of fruitless searching, Andrew and I went to the Mandurah boat show, the biggest in Western Australia. It seemed like it would be no different to any of the other boat shows we'd been visiting: we saw heaps, took our shoes off innumerable times … and then ended up at the catamarans. Might as well have a look!

The two of us went down the dock and the first thing we noticed was a Seawind 1000. We walked onto it. Andrew went to the left; I went to the right. We worked our way around, met up again in the middle and said nothing. Then he went to the right, I went to the left, and we met up back in the middle. Not a word was spoken. We left the boat, thanking the salesman as we exited, and went to the next one.

It was a Seawind 1200. We walked onto it. I went left; Andrew went right. Our paths crossed in the middle. He went left; I went right. Met in the middle and walked off.

By then there had been not a word spoken between us for some six or seven minutes. We walked in silence down the dock. Walked up the main pier. Stopped at the end. Turned and looked at each other.

'What do we do now?'

'We can't afford $600,000.'

'But that's the boat.'

'Yes, I know.'

'Let's find a cheaper version of *that* boat.'

'Right.'

We'd both settled on the Seawind 1200. Billed as a safe, tough, high-performance cruising yacht that allows you to travel the world with style and safety, it offered everything we'd ever wanted. It had a complete lounge room, with a table that didn't have to double as a bed; the galley was a similar size to an apartment kitchen; there were three good-sized bedrooms and a separate toilet and shower, so no hanging over the toilet to have a shower. In short, it was a compact holiday home.

* * *

Back we went to the 'net. There was nothing in WA, but we didn't give up. It took weeks, but we found her: *Windrider*, the prototype boat for the Seawind 1200, a Tony Grainger design G37, made of western red cedar and epoxy.

She was sitting in Port Hacking, south of Sydney, a little forlorn, painted a most unattractive grey, with pink and green stripes, like a pink and grey galah. Her owner was a Qantas flight attendant who'd had dreams of sailing her around the world, but time had made this too difficult for him. According to the advertisement, she had all the main basic stuff but had never been completed.

At the time, Andrew was flat out with work, so it fell to me to do the negotiating. The dealer was great. We had a lot of funny phone calls. Once he realised how serious we were about buying

Windrider, he tried to talk me out of the purchase. I remember standing at the phone with him saying, 'Don't do it. Can you imagine being out at sea for three or four days, never seeing land, and being totally alone and having to rely on no one but yourselves?'

It occurred to me that there was nothing I wanted more.

On my 37th birthday, I received a call from him telling me *Windrider* was ours. The perfect present.

Then it was Andrew's turn to worry. Whereas I had grown up sailing dinghies and felt confident we could handle it, Andrew had never really done much sailing. He didn't share my confidence. Two weeks later Andrew left to pick her up. My dad went with him, as I couldn't leave work and the kids at such short notice. The girls and I flew over to Mackay and met them there. Dad stayed with us until Cairns.

Andrew had been concerned I wouldn't like *Windie* when I actually saw her, but I fell in love with her immediately, horrible grey paint and all. Don't ask me why. She was a true renovator's dream. There was no flooring; we never did anything about that. The owner before us had painted himself into the middle of the back deck and had to walk out, so there were footprints in the paintwork. We never did anything about the footprints, either. But believe me, we did lots of other work.

It took four months for Andrew to sail her home, with me joining him whenever I could. One night I was on watch in the Torres Strait. It was 4am and I was getting sleepy, so I put on a favourite CD and went onto the back area and started dancing and singing along. Next to me I heard *pshew, pshew, pshew.* I looked down, and there was a pod of some 30 dolphins, not a metre from where I stood. They stayed with me until dawn. There was no sleeping after that!

* * *

Once we got *Windrider* home, there were a heck of a lot of things on the 'to do' list that would take us years, culminating in closing two businesses; painting the house, renting the house and moving out of the house; taking the kids out of school and linking them up with the School of Isolated and Distance Education, thanks to Deb, our wonderful teacher; and refitting the boat with new engines and everything else that spits and farts.

For four months before we left, Andrew worked full-time on the boat while I did the home stuff, all the while wondering if we were certifiable.

Eventually, we snuck out from Hillarys Boat Harbour on a blustery 1st July in 2009. We wanted to quietly slip away, as the build-up to leaving had been emotionally draining and overwhelming. Farewell parties, tears, advice, addresses — it was all a bit much. So it was only one old and dear friend who came alone to see us off, which somehow felt right.

We got about 1 nautical mile off our starting point when the autopilot misbehaved — our brand spanking new autopilot. I was so happy to be finished with all that farewelling, I would have volunteered to hand-steer to the North Pole if necessary.

But Andrew insisted on being sensible, and we dropped pick and made adjustments.

I had the horror of thinking we were going to have to do the whole leaving thing again! Luckily, 'twas not to be. In about an hour we were off. Phew. Hey, how 'bout that!

We were sailing off into the sunset. Cliché, here we come!

THREE

GETTING OUR SEA LEGS

Our trip took us from Perth, up the WA coast, along the Kimberleys to Darwin, where we spent three fantastic weeks having way too much fun. Darwinians are great! They are down-to-earth, friendly and generous people. We hadn't been there a day before we were offered a car to use, and then when Allan needed his car back, a new and wonderful friend, Louise, gave me her car each day with a time that 'madam' wished to be picked up. From there we would set off with her to the local watering hole and complete another spectacular day.

From Darwin, we set sail for Indonesia, opting to pick our way north via the remote eastern passage through Saumlaki. Generally speaking, we spent as much time ashore as we could. Our first taste of Indonesia was the very bustling city of Saumlaki. It was there we learned to tussle at the markets, which were located at the wharf; people would come each day with their fresh produce. We avoided the fish markets, which we named 'puke alley', due to the stench. At first we used our Bahasa Indonesia badly but soon we became proficientish at getting what or where we needed.

From Saumlaki, we headed north to the Banda group of islands, famed for their spices — they are the Spice Islands that made the Dutch rich in the 17th and 18th centuries. The whole area is scented with cloves, which dry on mats in front of the houses.

Banda is home to some of the most spectacular diving and snorkelling I have seen. One day we anchored the boat in 5 metres of water. While the bow of the boat was at 5 metres, the stern was in 500 metres! An amazing dropoff.

Bandaneira, the capital of the Banda group, boasts the live volcano Gunung Api, which is 666 metres high and consequently is known as the Devil's Peak. It is all scree and very difficult to climb. The girls and Andrew made it to the top, but I wimped out about three-quarters of the way up. Once they got back down, sliding all the way on their bums, they decided to go up again and stay the night. So off they went, with cans of baked beans and bedrolls, to sleep on a live volcano. Apparently it took three minutes to boil the baked beans by sitting them in the ground in a geyser.

From Banda it was further north to Ambon — not my favourite city. As adventures go, there was much about our time there that was grotty, filthy, putrid and frustrating. On one day that stays in my mind, we had to step over human faeces to get back to the dinghy, and then had to stop every 50 metres or so to remove a plakky bag or nappy wrapped around the propeller.

As luck would have it, we had to stay there three weeks, waiting on schoolwork and pain medication for Andrew, who broke three ribs when he slipped down the back steps.

One scary night in Ambon, we had to figure out what to do when a bunch of villagers came over to check us out and then wouldn't leave our boat. They sat there in the dark holding their machetes.

As we headed further north into New Guinea waters, this incident came to seem completely normal. Typically, we ran into problems in areas where it was hard to anchor, places where depths of up to 2000 feet were common. Then, anywhere the depth was manageable, there would be a village. Of course we would be a curiosity to the people, so they would always come to check us out and see what we could provide. This was usually medical aid or basic provisions.

Once, however, a man paddled out and asked us to follow him to shore. He had no Bahasa and only very basic English, so communication was a little difficult. He led us to a large shed filled with brown glass bottles and small brown sample bags of dirt. He pointed to the bottles and said, 'What?' We peered at them. The writing was in Chinese, but we made out 'HCL' on the sides. Yikes! We asked him if there had been any mining on the island, and yes, the Chinese had been nickel mining there six years before and had left, taking nothing with them. They had left behind thousands of these bottles. As best we could, we explained the danger, and he responded by showing us children who had been disfigured by the acid. What total lack of responsibility!

* * *

It was a magical sail heading for Palau. Light winds, sunshine — perfect. It took five nights and four days to get there, and we had day-long spinnaker runs. All the way, we were building Palau up to be this mythical dreamland, filled with all things not rice, egg and chicken, with all things 'unpoo' and clean, and we were concerned that no place could fulfil the Nirvana we had in mind.

We got into Palau at about 9am, cleared customs, and were pointed to 'Sam's' — never heard of it. As we pulled into a stunning anchorage with tall green mushroom islands, a dinghy sped out to meet us, and someone with a very slow southern US drawl said, 'Well, hello. You can park anywhere, use a mooring if you want, and the bar is over there.'

Ripper! We settled *Windie* and took off to find the bar.

At the shore end of two floating jetties sits Sam's. It's a dive operation, with bar, restaurant, gift shop, dive shop, underwater photography centre and internet café. After the squalor we'd come across in Indonesia, it was the Nirvana we were after, all by itself.

After we'd enjoyed about 10 minutes' peace, someone from immigration turned up wanting US$100. We didn't have any US dollars, and I hadn't had a chance to find out the location of the ATM, let alone get to it. The guy sitting opposite us, who had just introduced himself as Dennis, said, 'Here you go,' and gave the official the $100. That is, we were to find, typical of Palau. Before long, we'd also been befriended by Dennis's lovely wife, Carol. In short order, she bundled us into her car and gave us a guided tour. Dennis and Carol, it turns out, are yachties who arrived in Palau 13 years ago and had never got around to leaving.

We met lots of yachties at Sam's, people who were passing through and just happened to be there at that time, and a number of local yachties. Among them was Danny, an ex-US paramedic. By a stroke of luck, he happened to be right next to Diana when she was perched on the edge of the jetty at Sam's. When she leaned over to look at a photo, she fell into the water, knocking herself unconscious on the way down. Without blinking, he stripped off his dive gear and jumped in to rescue her. Thanks, Danny!

* * *

One morning, a few days into our stay on Palau, I was sitting at the bar sipping a coffee and a small, cheery man popped up and said, 'Hi, I'm Sam.' So began our friendship with Sam Scott, he of the 'Sam's' fame.

He has a brood of great kids, including the vivacious and engaging five-year-old Max, who once — in his enthusiasm to yell out '*Windrider*' to get our attention — fell off the jetty into the drink. We spent many days and attended many family events with Sam and his clan.

As we sat on Sam's balcony overhanging the water one Sunday afternoon, he said to me, 'Jen, you know you're part of the Sam's family now. You'll always be a part of us, and you'll always be welcome under our roof.'

Not surprisingly, our two planned weeks in Palau stretched out to four months. We loved the place and its people and made numerous friends there. So it was with tears all round that we eventually left, as time was not standing still waiting for us to get sick of Palau. By then we were six months into our planned two years away. It was time to move on.

FOUR

WEATHER

Weather, it has been said, is an inexact science, and it is something Andrew and I have always approached with the utmost caution. Between us, by this stage of our journey, we had notched up 65 years of boating experience — locally, nationally and now internationally — without getting into weather trouble. Determined not to be caught out — ever — we were relying not on one forecast for this region but several, putting the information together into an assimilation forecast. We were receiving weather reports daily, with a four-day outlook. All in all, we were never relying on one meteorological assessment, but six.

While on Yap, some 250 nautical miles northeast of our beloved Palau, we watched the weather carefully and waited until the forecasts consistently gave wind readings of 15 knots northeast. Only then did we set sail for Ulithi Atoll, 90 nautical miles northeast of Yap. It was approximately a day and a night's sail, so we planned to leave late morning with a view to arriving early the following morning.

About 20 nautical miles out of Yap, the weather forecast proved to be incorrect. A line of thunderies — storm clouds — followed us for the remaining 70 nautical miles. Shan chucked the whole way, which wasn't unusual for her. It was a very uncomfortable trip that we were glad to see the back of. However, once there, we anchored for the night and awoke to a tropical paradise.

It turned out we had anchored next to a beautiful coral island covered in palms and tropical vegetation, with a pristine beach, clear blue water, and — to complete the picture — I read out loud from an old copy of *The Coral Island* by R.M. Ballantyne. It was perfect. Idyllic. We swam, snorkelled, had the odd cold beverage and picked through the book, laughing with a kind of exhilaration at how much the descriptions related exactly to what was in front of us.

When we checked the weather that afternoon, we noted with concern that the low developing to the east of us appeared to be a potential typhoon: it started south of Pohnpei, the capital of Micronesia, and gradually moved to south of Chuuk, by which time it earned the name W98. It was described as a rain-bearing low, with winds up to 30 knots.

This was the forecast received that afternoon before the typhoon, 22nd March 2010. It warned of 'inclement weather' to come in and around our location:

[02W IS] THE FIRST TROPICAL DEPRESSION ... OF THIS
SEASON IN THE NW PACIFIC. ... THIS DEPRESSION
WILL CAUSE INCLEMENT WEATHER OVER KOROR AND
ESPECIALLY YAP FROM THIS EVENING INTO TUESDAY
AFTERNOON. LOCALLY HEAVY RAIN WITH WIND GUSTS
TO 35 KT ARE LIKELY FOR YAP DURING THIS PERIOD
... HIGH SURF ADVISORY IS INPLACED FOR THE EAST
FACING SHORES OF BOTH YAP AND PALAU AND WILL
REMAIN SO THRU TUESDAY NIGHT. THE COMBINATION
OF SWELLS AND WIND WAVES ASSOCIATED WITH 02W
CAN CAUSE SEA HEIGHTS TO REACH UP TO 13 FEET
TONIGHT INTO TUESDAY NIGHT.

Having tracked this for four days, we weren't convinced that it was going to be that low-key. We had watched the low start to spiral and gather strength and then appear more as a vortex on the radar. As a precaution, we moved to an island in the lee of the wind, anchored reasonably close to the shore and settled in. The island, named Sorelai, has a tiny itinerant population of about nine. We met a few villagers, who made us feel quite welcome.

After a dinner of beef curry, it was time for bed for the girls. Andrew and I made our preparations for what we thought was going to be a long night.

The next forecast predicted some rain, and winds at 25–30 knots, gusting up to 50. 'Okay,' we thought, 'we can handle that.'

We relayed the weather information to the islanders on neighbouring Mogmog, using VHF (very high frequency) radio.

Normally they would use HF (high-frequency) radio, but had lost this as the weather picked up. They had noticed us and thought we might be able to help with communications.

Next I caught up on some emails. My second-to-last was to my good friend Louise in Darwin. Coming from that neck of the woods, obviously she is a cyclone guru. I reported to her that if this was bad weather, it was all a bit of a beat-up. Ha! It would be a long time before I would hear from her again, much longer than anticipated.

Shortly after my 'beat-up' email, I was eating my words. The wind began picking up to a consistent 50, then 60, knots. Then the anchor dragged, so we began a long night of resetting the anchor as it dragged in coral over sand. After about four resets, the wind began gusting over 80 knots and sitting steadily around 68 knots. The sky was wildly alight as lightning danced around the clouds surrounding us. It was eerie and scary. Not happy, Jan.

By the wee tiny hours of morning, we were recording gusts of over 90 knots and were in contact with the islanders, as they still had no communications. They reported damage, and we reported our anchor situation.

An email expressing concern came in from our Palau-based friend Jay, in the Philippines, who was watching the weather on radar. Jay is best mates with Dennis, and the pair have taken it upon themselves to help any yachtie or islander in distress in the region. They also know where to source anything at all for yachts in Palau. They can almost always be found in the mornings at

Sam's bar, having a coffee together and sharing a laugh with anyone who stops by.

> Hey! ... ummmm ... storm looking kinda close to y'all. You guys ok?
> Any drama/excitement?
> Hope all is well enough but not boring!
> Jay

* * *

> Thanks for your concern.
> Last gust 87kn ...
> not happy
> keep you posted
> glad u know where we are
> Cheers

* * *

> two words — fuck me! when your hands are not full let us know all ok, eh?
> hunker down. hang on,
> J

According to the Beaufort scale of wind-strength measurement, the oft-cited Force 10 gale is 52 knots. This is classified as a storm. Force 12 is the highest measure on this scale. Classified as a hurricane, it is pinned at 64–71 knots, with probable wave heights of 13.7 metres and maximum wave heights of 15.8 metres. I didn't know that at the time, but thinking about it since, it reassures me that our reactions on the night were totally justifiable. The written transcript of forecasts received that night on the HF stated that the weather system was a 'marginal tropical storm', and the winds would be of a maximum consistent strength of 30 knots.

When the anchor dragged again, we decided to put out the other anchor, with a much longer line. That was like getting out on the front of a car as you fly along the freeway at 110 kilometres an hour. In fact 110km/h is about 55 knots, and we were in much stronger winds, but you can start to imagine what we experienced getting out that second anchor. Once that step was accomplished, we felt more comfortable.

Having said that, Andrew got the para-anchor and life raft ready, just in case. Good move; the anchor held for about five hours, then we were unexpectedly on the move, not knowing if the anchor was dragging or if the line had snapped. We were at the mercy of the wild whipping waves again.

When we tried to reset the second anchor, again back at the bow of the boat — yikes, another trip up the motorway on the bonnet of a speeding car — we realised that the line had snapped. No more second anchor.

It was now daybreak. It's true that all seems better in the daylight, but the situation was also much clearer and somehow more real. We got the kids up super fast — no time to get dressed even — and into their PFDs (personal flotation devices). The kids were fantastic and just did what we asked of them. We were by this stage too involved to feel the enormity of what was happening.

Next we discovered that, during the night, the main halyard (the line that hoists the sail) had unfurled off its cleat at the base of the mast and found its way behind the boat and around both propellers. Had we realised this in the night, that would have made the difference, I think. We radioed the village, explained our predicament and said we were on the way towards them. We were adrift, with no means to control the boat, but our trajectory put us on Mogmog.

They apologised and said they couldn't help. That wasn't a shock! We were battling! What were *they* supposed to do in dugout canoes?

In desperation, we tried to start both engines and, inevitably, nothing happened, thanks to the halyard strangling the propellers. Andrew wanted to go over the side of the boat and try to cut away the halyard. At this point the sterns (the rear ends of the hulls) were slapping about 2 feet under the water and rising 4 feet above it. There was no way Andrew was going over; it was totally unsafe. I had enough on my plate without trying to drag an unconscious 100-kilogram blob out of the water in 180-kilometre-an-hour winds! So we decided that if we had to choose what to abandon — the boat or us — it would have to be the boat.

FIVE

READY OR NOT, MOGMOG HERE WE COME

We were drifting rapidly towards Mogmog. We could see the villagers running along the shore, calling and gesticulating. Was this a good thing or a bad thing? We had no way of knowing.

I yelled to the kids to grab the really important stuff, then shoved wallets, passports, our permits and immigration file, keys and a few other essentials into a large waterproof bag. At the same time, Andrew was running around like a headless chook deploying the para-anchor. Predictably, the kids came back with their favourite stuffed toys, so into the bag they went.

All of us checked our PFDs and made sure we had our handheld VHF and personal EPIRBs (emergency position-indicating radio beacons).

Next thing, we ran into a line of breakers over a sandbar, about 700 metres from shore. 'Brace yourselves.'

It was, naturally, at this moment that the primary anchor grabbed. Fantastic! We were now caught on a sandbar 700 metres off the island.

We saw two lines of waves converging on the sandbar, each coming from 45-degree angles in front of us. This resulted in a curling wave coming directly on the nose. The waves were towering above us. We lay on the floor of the cockpit and watched through the windows as a wall of water built and then curled over us — it must have been about 9 metres in height. As if in slow-motion, the water came down and crashed on the coachroof and windows. The boat lurched and tossed as we braced for the next equally high wave.

The sound of the waves hitting the deck had become so disturbing, we wondered how long the boat could survive such a pounding. *Windrider's* bow was quite literally through the waves, and by the time each wave broke on top of us, it was a foaming wall of green.

There was a sudden awful noise from the foredeck, but we had absolutely no idea what it was. Then the boat lurched harder and further, and we were moving again. Later we worked out that the commotion from the bow was the sound of the windlass (the device for winding the anchor) smashing through the deck under the incredible strain being provided by the anchor. At the same time the windlass gave way, the anchor chain broke, and all the stainless steel shackles keeping it in place were snapped and straightened. We surged towards the island.

'Let's get the dinghy in the water,' Andrew shouted over the howling wind.

I shook my head.

To me, it made better sense to be in something big rather than a flimsy dinghy, and Andrew was soon convinced, so we stayed on our stricken catamaran. But then we became concerned about the treatment *Windie* was going to get when she inevitably slammed into the beach. At about 100 metres offshore, we inflated our life jackets and jumped into the dinghy. Andrew stayed in the water to hold down the windward side of the dinghy to stop it capsizing.

* * *

All the way from the Philippines, our friend Jay was cheering us on, but we had no way of knowing that at the time.

hey ... you in the clear?

All web info saying never over 50kn gusts.

Ha! Maybe they should've stayed the night with you guys.

Anyway, hope you held and all ok.

Let us know or we'll have to start organizing Operation Save-Wombats.

* * *

Ok ... too long no reply ... you kids ok?

— Jay

Waves crashed over us, but we made it safely to shore. Immediately, women from the village swept up Shannon and Diana and then they all vanished. Others indicated for me to follow them, but no way was I going to miss the final act! Andrew was surrounded by men in loincloths, and the boat was crashing. The girls were safe. What would you do?

As I watched from the beach, the men from Mogmog tried to get lines to *Windrider* but couldn't. Sticking out into the water were the remains of two jetties built by US soldiers during World War II. Time had reduced them to metal shards pointing skywards. The men tried desperately to stop the boat landing on this metallic war junk, but the weather had other plans. Before my eyes, *Windie* was can-opened right down the starboard hull in great jagged holes. Very disappointing. She finally came to rest on the beach, with surf pounding her and, instantly, about a hundred Mogmog men started climbing all over her. Andrew was in there trying to help, but the inexorable wind had other ideas.

Given that my world had just been turned on its head, it would've been good to reflect a bit at this point, to have thought what to do next, but forget that! Villagers were poring over our badly damaged boat and, as one, they decided to get everything off it.

With all the men helping, they took everything to a nearby building that turned out to be the dispensary. Right; better follow! Andrew stayed with the boat, never knowing if these men were helping us or stealing. Beer was flowing. One man was even wearing Andrew's shorts! At this point, we were pretty much along for the ride.

By the time I arrived, our 'stuff' was strewn all over the building's wide verandah. I was relieved to see that Shannon and Diana had been taken there earlier and were being looked after by the women.

Actually, the men didn't quite take everything to the dispensary. We'd had quite a lot of beer stowed. This they drank. Every last drop. Cold or warm. It was a real party atmosphere. There was even a sense of hysteria — or was that me? Probably me.

Somebody introduced Andrew and me to the chief, a dignified man named Juanito. He graciously informed us that there was a house available for us to live in.

Our heads were spinning; we just nodded numbly and thanked him very much. Up until an hour or so before, we'd had a magnificent home, and now it was stuck out in the water like a bird with a damaged wing. It was numbness that I felt at this point, and a feeling of surreal helplessness overlaid with a sense that it would all be okay if I just went with the flow.

A coffee was thrust into my hand and a sarong supplied — by I know not whom. Shan was spirited off somewhere for a shower and Diana was being fussed over, so I was free to go and check on what remained of the boat. I trudged back the 75 metres or so, keen to see what was happening.

This was when I came face to face with the wilder side of Mogmog. The side where if an item isn't tied down, it'll be off and in someone's house before you can blink. Actually, that's not quite right: if it *is* tied down, nailed down, screwed in, installed or in any way a part of anything, it will still disappear. As I reached *Windrider*, by now lying half submerged on the beach, one man was going for the solar panels. When I stopped him, he told me they were cracked, so he was removing them.

'No way, Sunshine! Get off here *now!*' I said, fairly animatedly. The panels were, of course, okay. And then I mentally took stock and realised I was treading a very fine line, and that while I needed to preserve what I could, I also needed to placate and smooth the way with these men.

* * *

In the course of our rescue, we saw the worst and best the people of Mogmog had to offer: outright thievery and lying and also incredible kindness and deep religious faith. The women — strong and generous — went to church to pray for us and scattered ash into the ocean to calm the waves. They were wonderful to the girls, and that's when I knew that the women of Mogmog, generally speaking, have a huge sense of family.

By juxtaposition, I was very unsure of the men's intentions.

SIX

SITTING AND TAKING STOCK

Later that day, when all our gear had been moved to the house Juanito so kindly made available to us, we finally drew breath.

Together, all four of us sat on the beach surveying our much-loved *Windrider*. Here we were, a long way from anywhere, our dreams probably in tatters, in a place where we knew nothing of the culture or language. What were the logistics we needed to deal with? What did our future hold?

Physically, we were amazingly unharmed. The kids had a couple of superficial scratches. But in terms of shock and upset, how were we holding up? Some people would say we'd been lucky to escape with our lives. Were we traumatised by what we'd been through earlier that day? No.

I have heard it said, and by now it was also my experience, that when you live through something like a shipwreck, everything happens so fast that you only have time to think very specifically in the immediate short term, and to plan in the slightly longer short term. Decisions must be immediate, and often two of you must come to the same conclusion or defer to the other very quickly. There is no time for argument. Every moment must be used positively.

Fortunately, the kids had done exactly what was asked of them, down to jumping into the dinghy naked except for PFDs and sluicing vomit off themselves as we made for shore. They are very self-sufficient little beings, so needed only minimal direction from us.

As for Andrew and me, we have been together, working together and second-guessing each other for more than 30 years. For us there have never been set roles in boat handling. Whoever is there makes the decisions. This meant we were able to work independently together, if that makes any sense, and there was never disagreement. In hindsight, in regards to all that had happened to this point, there is nothing — other than noticing the damned broken halyard — that I would've done differently.

Back to the present, though: where the fuck are we again? Where exactly is Mogmog?

For the navigationally interested, it's at about 10°N, 140°E. That puts it at almost the western end of Yap State. The nearest centre, Yap, is 90 nautical miles southwest of here. Yap has two supermarkets with basic facilities, a few hotels, and it feels like a country beach-holiday town. You can get pretty much anything you need for normal life, but not what you might want. And certainly not what you need to carry out what amounts to a complete hull rebuild!

Courtesy of our rescuers, a lot of items seemed to have been whisked away. We didn't know where the iPod had got to but we did have the leads. We needed to make a list and try to track down all the other bits and pieces. At this point we seemed light-handed in terms of our equipment, but had yet to take stock.

Our plan? To do as we had always done. Work it out together. Whatever course that might take. There were no immediate plans, just a sense of being in the moment and not knowing where that moment might lead. Surreal is such an overused word, but nothing else seemed to really fit.

* * *

Sitting down made us realise how bone-tired we were. It'd be so good to stretch out and sleep. But first we needed to sort out where, and get bedding organised before the dust — or was that coral? — settled on this long, long day.

Our new abode was just 25 metres from the dispensary. My first impression was that it was damp and dark.

The girls and I and various helpful souls had spent much of the afternoon transferring our possessions the short distance from the dispensary verandah to the house. As it had become apparent to us that if an item wasn't taken from the boat to the house, it would just be straight taken, I became a bit more circumspect. From that point on I requested the return of specific items, and prioritised things like the kids' toys and schoolwork, my beloved flute, the hand-carved wooden jewellery box Dad brought home for me from Italy when I was eight, and the carved wooden treasure-chest jewellery box that Andrew made for Shan when *she* was eight. In this, we were successful, as long as we nominated particular items, but given that there was — especially to the islanders — a heck of a lot of gear, I still lost track of things.

Before long, the only people in the house besides us were Tess, the daughter of the principal of the school, and Catherine, a Peace Corps worker who had been living on Mogmog for almost two years. They explained how for decades, the United States had been sending young US Peace Corps workers to the island to carry out varying roles. Catherine was a teacher's aide in the States and is employed as a teacher on the island. Tess and she have formed a strong friendship. The girls insisted on sweeping the place clean and tidying up before they headed home. Home for Peace Corp workers is with a sponsored family, a little further west on the island.

* * *

Andrew had returned to *Windrider* to try to figure out the extent of the damage. When I ducked back to see how he was getting on, it was mayhem! It was as if the earlier party at the dispensary had popped back up on *Windrider*. Everywhere I looked I saw local men dressed in their traditional thus (pronounced thooz). These are long strips of cloth wound in a certain, quite complicated way, to be a loincloth cum wraparound skirt. The torso is always naked. Women in Mogmog, I'd noticed, don't wear tops either, just a lavalava, which is a hand-woven wraparound skirt with horizontal stripes. And that's it. No tops at all.

The boat was thus full of thus, and men drinking every last drop of our beer. And the wine. And the vodka. And the scotch. And rummaging through all the hatches, cupboards and hidey holes, ostensibly getting stuff out for us.

While the local men enjoyed the festivities, Andrew and I were slipping and slithering on diesel-smeared bits of boat, trying to assess damage. The starboard hull was full of water up to the bedroom. It seriously looked like something from a *Titanic* set. Water was thigh-deep that side, and the floor was buckled, with coral and sand washing up through gaping holes in the hull. Our bedroom at the front of the boat was pretty much awash. What we didn't realise at that point is the hull underneath the buckled floor was completely gone, so that in times to come we would look through the removed floor to see the coral beneath.

We let the men finish off the beer and tried to save the remainder of our possessions. People we did not yet know were making off with our frozen goods, rather than letting them go to waste. It was all a slightly hysterical blur.

When nothing remained, they all left.

We went to the house.

* * *

For the first time since our abrupt arrival, we were left alone as a family. Second impression of the house? Damp and dark.

One fluorescent light hung in the main room. Fishing line was strung across at intervals to hang washing from. Aaaah, *that's* the damp — all our stuff hanging there.

Beyond the main room, which was concreted — floor, walls and ceilings — was a hallway. First door left opened onto a storage room; second door left opened onto the bathroom.

The bathroom had no light, one non-flushing toilet, and a 44-gallon drum lined with plastic stood in the corner. This was half-filled with not-so-clear water and sported half a cordial bottle to use as a scoopy thing. Over this was a PVC tube connected to a tap outlet with no tap handle, just the spindle. Out with the pliers for that one. More clothes were hanging from fishing line. The whole bathroom was awash with water of unknown source.

On the right of the hall was a sort of small empty bedroom. Upstairs, there were three bedrooms on the left and at the top of the stairs, on the right, an open room. The roof leaked. There were puddles throughout the second floor.

Juanito popped in to see how we were getting on and also to advise Andrew to sleep on the boat. If he didn't, the chief said, all the fittings would be stripped out of it by morning.

Next a group of quite merry young men came by asking Andrew to go with them to drink tuba (pronounced tooba). This is a potent mix from the flower of coconut trees. Harvest it in the morning and it's ready to go that night. Waste not, want not! By this time, it was about 8pm.

Andrew decided to go for a while, figuring that being sociable was probably a good thing right now.

Our next visitor was a quietly spoken 55-year-old woman named Alberta. I was to discover that Alberta is a gem, as so many of these Mogmog women are. In she came and sat down. She looked around carefully, taking in every detail. In the eyes of the villagers, we must have an obscene amount of stuff — even though by the time Alberta saw us, we had been relieved of so much! She asked where Andrew was. I told her.

'They are not your friends. Be careful,' she said.

Although I pressed her to explain, she wouldn't elaborate. As I got to know her better, I would learn that Alberta is always careful in her choice of words.

Before going, she asked what we needed. I answered that we were fine and just needed a bit of time to think and adjust. Nodding, she suggested I turn off the light if I wanted peace.

* * *

Presumably I did something about dinner that night but I don't remember. The girls and I arranged mattresses on the floor and they got ready for bed. Andrew had taken what he needed to spend the night on the boat.

Do you know what? His absence turned out to be the hardest part of that day. It hit me like a ton of bricks that what I needed most of all right then was to be with Andrew — to chat, vent and certainly not sleep.

But, for the sake of peace and a semblance of normality for the girls, out went the light and the long night began.

SEVEN

LEARNING THE RHYTHMS OF MOGMOG

At 6am, 6.30, and 6.50 respectively, a harsh clangy bell rang, ushering in our first full Mogmogian day. Every day here begins with the church bell, we now know. We also know that our new abode is the visiting priest's house, so guess where the church is? Yup! Right next door. Fantastic!

Andrew came through the door looking not too bad. Fortunately for him, there'd been no visitors.

Soon after, Alberta arrived with a huge bunch of bananas. Gratitude just doesn't do justice to how I feel about her gesture, or towards her. Funny how fast you can become fond of someone.

Andrew focused on assessing the boat, and I turned my attention to the house. The kids met the island kids, of which there seem to be hundreds.

I took a walk around the immediate vicinity. It's a very pretty island. There are frangipani trees everywhere, and not just white-flowered ones. They range from the deepest magenta to the purest white. The whole island is perfumed by them. Wandering around I bumped into Juanito, who was surveying the storm damage. Coconut palms had been ripped out by their root balls; banana vines were bent in rows at 90 degrees; papaya trees were basically moosh. He bemoaned the likelihood that by the time the insurance assessor made it to Mogmog, there would be no evidence of the damage.

'Why don't you take photos?'

'We have no camera.'

'I do ... I'll take them and meet with the assessor.'

'Really? Wow.'

Photos taken, I wandered back to the house. My aim was to put everything as 'away' as possible when you have no shelves or cupboards. One corner of the main room I requisitioned as a pseudo kitchen. Everything kitcheny I stacked on a metal desk, with the butane single burner hotplate to cook on in pride of place.

Mid-morning, Juanito came by with a thermos of hot water, with instructions to keep it for future use. In the afternoon, he popped back with an ice-cooler drink bin full of ice and told us to come each day for a refill. Funny how he knew that the simple things make the biggest difference.

Alberta spent much of that day with me, teaching me, advising me. She continued to help me; often, in the weeks and months ahead, she would pop in with bananas and a smile, typically with four or five grandkids in tow.

At this early stage we still had pretty much all the food from the boat, so supplies weren't a problem. Unknown to me, Raymond, who we were yet to really know, had taken all our frozen goods and stored them for us in his freezer.

Around 8pm, the house started to fill up with visitors, all men, and all apparently with a skinful of tuba. The men seemed to want to sit and chat. I did my best to be polite and sat and chatted, not knowing if that was the right thing to do. When I mentioned to the saintly Alberta that I had had enough, she took on the role of bouncer and tipped them all out.

With the girls asleep for the night on the mattress and Alberta, having played shepherd, now back in her own home, finally Andrew and I were left to sit and talk. Things had evolved so that, after going about our largely independent days, we now had a functioning house, albeit with no toilet paper, and we knew we could manage fine, thanks to Juanito's generosity and Alberta's diplomatic interventions.

Andrew had been taking the first bite of the elephant. He could have done with somebody like Alberta at his side, someone to talk with about removing the engines once the boat was out of the surf line. But Andrew isn't into navel-gazing, and although he was on his own, he got stuck in. He had spent the day securing lines to the boat and trying to work out if the boat could be dragged from the water. He had decided on a flowchart. If the boat could be dragged from the water, and if the engines could be salvaged, then there could be more flowchart. If not, then salvage was unfeasible.

It wasn't necessary that night for Andrew to sleep on the boat. It was good to be under one roof. Night-night, Mogmog.

* * *

The next day dawned clear, almost as a mockery of what had come before. Motivated and a bit refreshed from a not altogether sleepless night, after breakfast we all set to work. Andrew headed down to the boat to work out a way to get her up the beach. To do this she had to come up a 20-degree incline on hard coral scree. Chook, that's Diana, sorted out the room down the hall, commandeering it for the girls' cave.

Ripper! I found a spotlight, so I did a bit of a swap-around. Out went the fluoro in the main room, and in went the spotty. Voilà! The toilet has a light!

Unusually, we were collecting our thoughts when Raymond arrived. Raymond is Juanito's non-appointed 2IC. An intensely intelligent, self-taught man, he runs the town generator and everyone's power; he is, hence, a whiz with all things diesel and also all things electronic. He has a wag of a wife, named Jolene, and three lovely kids. Hugely generous with his possessions and his time, every night he uses his TV outside so everyone can watch it. Kids' TV first, then kids to bed, and then adult stuff. He is a strong personality, widely respected in the village, and has a devilish sense of humour. For me, his reputation preceded him because he and Andrew had become instant friends.

Anyway, I digress. Raymond told us we had a power point.

'Really?'

'240 volts.'

'Really?'

'Here it is.'

Fuck me. It's an *Australian plug*! What are the chances?

Raymond watched us, bemused, as we ran around like idiots, with extension leads, power boards, microwave, lights. And, guess what, we were able to hook up the microwave, light in the kids' room, computer charging, satellite-phone charging, leads everywhere.

Home at last!

EIGHT

THE VILLAGE VERSUS THE BOAT

An old scuba bottle hangs from a tree in the open space in the middle of the village. A few times I had wandered past it without a thought. Then, on the afternoon of our third day on Mogmog, two men start banging it with metal tubing. 'Why?' thinks I.

In response to the loud clanging, men, women and children come from everywhere, and we Barries are among them. Juanito is officiating, and he orders everyone down to where *Windrider* is lying half in and half out of the surf line. In next to no time, two very long ropes are attached to the front of the boat and perhaps 200 people have fanned out around her, knee-deep in the water, ready to try to heave her up the beach.

With one of the men leading the chant, we all tugged the boat, and tugged and tugged. It was about 3.30pm when the effort started, and Juanito called it stumps at six. During that time, I never heard a complaint. People were laughing and joking, both with me and among themselves. It really made me think. Where in Western 'civilisation' would you find 200 strangers willing to pull their guts out for you for two and a half hours, all the time maintaining good humour? Answer: nowhere, that's where.

You know how far we moved the boat? Not a millimetre. Not one.

Andrew and I tried very hard to maintain positivity that night. We had decided that if the boat couldn't be dragged from the water, then we couldn't remove and then assess the engines. If this could not be done, then the engines could not even be replaced, and we would be heading back home without *Windie* and the lifestyle that we loved so much.

Next day, *clang, clang, clang* on the scuba bottle again, and it was back to the job for the same 200 or so smiling people. This time, the men had managed to get hold of a chain block, from Raymond's power house. We all lined up and resumed the tugging. From my spot on the rope, when I looked around it was impossible to see both ends of the line. That gives the perspective of the number of people there helping. Right up the front were the younger men, pulling like all get out. After them were the older men, the leaders of the village, who were planning and thinking in their breaks from pulling. Next there were all the boys and girls, yelling as they pulled, and then behind me, all the women, alternately pulling and laughing, breasts flying everywhere. It was quite a sight.

After heaving for two hours, we had managed to pull the boat forwards by about an inch.

After calling it quits for the day, the older men continued talking. Apparently there was another chain block on a nearby island. They organised to get it here so we could do it all again. Juanito suggested siphoning the fuel out of *Windrider*, to remove excess weight. This was done straight away, and Andrew and some others went over the boat once again, removing yet more things in order to reduce the load.

Andrew spent the next day digging out under the hulls to change the angle we were pulling, as the beach angle was about 20 degrees, and we hadn't taken account of that discrepancy. That took the whole day.

Then *clang, clang, clang* went the scuba bottle again, and to my amazement, the villagers all came to the beach *again*! This time we had progress! We managed to pull *Windrider* about a metre. Not far at all but at least a sign that we *might* be able to do this.

While I listened to the elders mooting about the next step to take, it struck me that if this scenario was taking place in Australia, by now we would have had arguments as to how the task should be undertaken. Way too many chiefs and nowhere near enough Indians. Not on Mogmog. Here, someone suggests an approach, they all listen, they work out how to implement it, and see if it works. If it does, good; if it doesn't, the next suggestion will come forward, and so on. This particular moot was about borrowing yet another — much larger — chain block from Falalop.

Falalop, an island 5 nautical miles away, is home to the area high school, post office, airport (such as it is), and a few houses that double as shops. The high school kids go there every Monday morning by dinghy and come home Friday afternoon. So radio contact was made to confirm availability, and then when the school kids left the following Monday (as everywhere, with their mothers waving them off), the chain block came back with the dinghy.

Andrew took advantage of the couple of days' delay to do more digging. By now he was really feeling burdened by the fact that everyone was going to so much effort on our behalf. He felt obliged to work his butt off.

I couldn't help him with the digging, as Mogmogian women are not supposed to sweat. It is forbidden and highly frowned upon for women to do physical work. I guess rope-pulling comes into the fun category. So all I could do was play support crew: keep the food and water coming and keep the kids out of the way and gainfully occupied. I figured that I needed to toe the line and be as unobtrusive as possible.

Andrew rapidly reached a point where he was suffering from heat exhaustion, and then got the runs from the water. It's not that it's particularly hot. The temperature sits at a pretty even 31 degrees, but the humidity is up there, and with constant physical activity the sweat just pours out.

One thing that should be said is that when Andrew takes on a task, he will work for 10 to 12 hours without a break, except for water or food that I bring down and he eats. If I didn't do that he would just keep going.

The kids came down with the runs, too. So it wasn't a fun weekend, especially as the toilet doesn't flush, we had no loo paper left, and there was none to be had on the island. I didn't want to think about what *that* meant. For the time being, we had to resort to the kids' old schoolwork for loo paper. Not good, but what do you do? It did prompt Andrew to say he was becoming a real smart arse. Yeah … bit late for that one, methinks! We worked out that if you poured 5ish litres of water down the loo, it will sort of flush. Sounds easy, but the water comes from our one water tank, which is rain-supplied, so when that's gone, that's it. So far, so good.

Andrew's urine had become dark brown, despite drinking about 10 litres of fluid each day. All weekend, he pretty much slept and drank and did nothing else. By Monday, he was feeling better, and his wee was a healthier colour.

When the scuba bottle was clanged at about 4pm on Monday, I thought that no one would come. Wrong! Come, they did, all 200 of them, and their attitude had subtly changed. Now it was, 'We're going to beat this boat.'

'The village will not be beaten.'

'We don't have machines, but we have people.'

'We'll get everyone from the other islands if we need to.'

'Don't give up hope, it *will* happen; we will make it happen.'

These are all direct quotes from people who spoke to me that day. For the first time since all this began, I was close to tears.

So we all pulled again, and the boat moved. It really moved. It really instantly and appreciably moved! That was it. The tears were there this time.

We pulled and pulled and *Windrider* came to rest about 3 metres further up the beach. Everyone was elated, but buggered. Not there yet, but the task was doable, and nearly done.

Next day, there was no clanging. Andrew had dug new tracks for the hulls, and he and the guys helping him thought they might be able to finish the job using only the chain blocks. They had had to take pressure off one of the blocks by tying it around the men's rest room on the beach. I had visions of it flying away into the surf with a startled occupant still on the throne.

Even though there was no scuba clang, about 80 people were on hand to haul the boat the remaining distance. And we did it. Finally *Windrider* was right off the beach and into the trees. As far as she could go.

The village had won. Just as they had said they would. Another bite of elephant chewed and swallowed.

* * *

Since this all began, I have looked very hard at my own 'civilised' culture. I have to say that we Westerners are unbelievably up ourselves to think of ourselves as superior in *any* way to other cultures. Using Mogmog as an example, these people are happy, educated, funny, generous, community-minded and spirited, living the life they choose. Many kids go to school in Chuuk or the United States and freely opt to come back and live here.

I have never seen a more functional team in operation. The people of Mogmog choose to maintain traditional gender roles because it works and they are happy with them. At the same time, they respect our ways, and ask only that we respect theirs.

However, this is easier said than done, and the whole topless thing was becoming an issue. Catherine came to tell me that the villagers would respect my wish to wear clothes, but if I was to be part of the community, then I really needed to abide by their traditional dress code. She had been topless herself since arriving.

This really goes against the grain for me. So it was with much chagrin that I doffed the tops and tried to assimilate with the locals. Andrew thought it was hilarious. I was very uncomfortable.

NINE

THE ART OF SOURCING SUPPLIES IN MICRONESIA

SOOOO sorry to hear about your recent fate on the great ocean waves. Lesser human beings would throw up their hands, curse everyone and everything and head for home in comfort. Not you mob! And unless you are keeping it secret squirrel, I am presuming that your fabulous family unit is still intact. Glad not to hear any report of personal physical or emotional damage ...

You're a tough bunch, and to be admired

Love and luck with the rebuild and the rats,

Louise XXXX

Next tasks: remove engines, assess engines and organise supplies. Three guesses who got what when the jobs were divvied up!

It took Andrew a day and a half to get the engines out. He block-and-tackled them out through the hatches he had made in the deck, just in case — Captain Anal. He made up an engine stand from some wood Juanito found for him. Worked a treat.

Andrew and Raymond, Juanito's '2IC', worked on the engines. This sounds corny, but it was a big step. Suddenly Andrew had his version of Alberta. The pair seemed to forge an effortless friendship and there were huge laughs. I'm not sure they are good for each other, as they have the same devilish humour, and I can forsee a fair few tuba escapades happening, but they seem to have a lot of fun in each other's company.

They stripped the starter motors, alternators and all the other bits and pieces and started to rebuild them from scratch. Other village men came and went with their suggestions. It was a hugely positive time.

* * *

Meanwhile, from Raymond, I discovered that there was a ship coming this way from Yap so I needed to get my skates on and make sure we had an order placed. Fresh supplies! Alcohol, for sanity purposes! Andrew started dreaming of boat parts; me of toilet paper. The girls were more keen to establish friendships with the myriad kids on the island, than to worry about food. The aim of the game was to organise our much-needed supplies to go from the stores in Yap onto the ship in time for the shipping guys to do whatever they needed to do, and then to get it to the correct island, and for it to be the correct stuff. Right! I can do that!

Not being au fait with island life, figuring out how to make this happen was a bit scary. And I was tight for time. It was now

Tuesday. The ship was leaving Friday and needed to be loaded on Thursday. In less than three days I had to work out how to order, pay and co-ordinate shipping. Aaaahh!

I prepared myself for a session on the phone. Our satellite phone works okay before 10am and after 4pmish. Figure this out: it's a sat phone but you have to dance all over the place to get reception — under that tree, in that sunny place, over there … no … no … over there. And we're talking satellites! Why it should be like this is beyond me! On top of that there is a significant delay between vocalising and being heard. It's maybe two seconds. And, if you talk on top of the other person, neither of you hears anything.

Rang the hardware store first and ascertained that the hardware and the general store were one company. Good start. One office, one set of accounts. Fantastic. I rang the shop: 00116913502209.

'Could I speak to someone in accounts, please?'

'Hold on.'

'Okay.'

Enter 'Home on the Range' clunky music-box-style hold music, which over the sat phone becomes wonderfully distorted.

Eventually … 'Hello.'

'Hello, could I speak to someone in accounts, please?'

'No.'

'Are they not there?'

'Pardon, I cannot hear you,' and the phone cuts out.

'Hello.'

'Hello.'

'Could I have accounts, please?'

'Hold on … Hello.'

'Hello. Could you tell me who handles the accounts there, please?'

'Yes. That is Ali.'

'Thank you. Is Ali there?'

'No, ring back in an hour.'

'Okay. Thank you.'

Hmmm … an hour is getting close to 10am and that's when the phone starts cutting out.

* * *

10am. I dial 00116913502209.

'Hello, is Ali there, please?'

'Hold on.' More 'Home on the Range'.

'Hello.'

'Hello.'

'Is Ali there, please?'

'No.'

'I was asked to ring back at this time to talk to him.'

'Ring back in an hour.'

'Is there anyone else who might be able to help me set up an account?'

'No.'

'Okay, I'll ring back.'

Rang back in an hour and couldn't get through, and couldn't get through and couldn't get through until at the predictable 4pm, by which time the staff were finishing up for the day.

Very, very frustrating.

* * *

By 5pm, Andrew and Raymond had alternater and starter-motor bits everywhere and were in reconstruct mode. They were very happy with themselves.

All in all, we'll call that a good day.

* * *

Okay, now it's Wednesday.

00116923502209.

'Hello.'

'Hello. Is Ali there, please?'

'Hold on.'

'Home on the Range' again.

'Hello.'

'Hello. Is Ali there?'

'No, he will be here in an hour.'

Sense of déjà vu happening here. 'Okay, I'll ring back in an hour.'

That put it at 8.30, so nowhere near 10 o'clock. Good start, Jen.

I ring the hardware store to hopefully place an order. Only one guy there speaks fluent English. His name is Sam.

I have shortened this exchange to spare you another four frustrating calls. Eventually Sam assures me he has four 4-ton hydraulic jacks, so we can lift the boat. Great. I also order some timber and hexagonal nuts and bolts to make up a structure for the boat to rest on as it is being jacked.

It was a good conversation, which only left for the account to be organised.

* * *

00116913501109. By now I have this number memorised!

'Hello.'

'Hello.'

'Is Ali there, please?'

'Hang on.'

'Home on the Range' *again.*

'Hello.'

'Hello. Is Ali there, please?'

'No, he has left for the day.'

'But it's only 8.30!'

'Yes, he has left for the day.'

'Can anyone else *please* help me set up an account?'

'Yes, Susan can.'

Aaaahhh! 'Is Susan there, please?'

'Yes.'

'Great.'

'Hello.'

'Hello.'

'Is that Susan?'

'Yes.'

'Great. Can I organise an account with you?'

'Yes.'

Hooray! After another four calls, with the phone dropping in and out, we get the account established.

'Right, can I now place an order to go on the ship on Friday?'

'No, you will have to wait for Ali to do that tomorrow.'

'That's Thursday, and the boat must be loaded on Thursday afternoon.'

'It will be fine.'

'Okay. Thank you.'

* * *

More than a little sceptical, I ring Sam back and tell him the account details. He assures me he will have someone named Dan sitting on our hardware stuff on the ship so it won't get stolen.

Theft is a huge issue, I am told. The ship is notorious for having goods stolen while in transit. Naturally, no one ever knows who has stolen whatever it is or where it might have ended up!

* * *

Andrew and Raymond have managed to get the starboard engine started and purring!

When they told me that, I lost it a bit; not in a screaming, shouting sort of way, but I couldn't speak while I fought back tears. On one hand we were elated about the rapid progress with the engine, and on the other, frustrated at the prospect of perhaps getting no food, toiletries, boat repair supplies and what have you.

Big deep breaths and I pull myself together. All in all, still have to call it a great day.

* * *

Thursday.

00116913502209.

Got hold of Ali — fantastic. He told me the account was sorted and I could place the shop order with Dominic. He was incredibly patient. The phone continually cut out over 45ish minutes while Ali painstakingly took down the order, but he was wonderful.

I ended that phone call frustrated but happy.

Next having rung the hardware shop once more to confirm everything was on track, and being told Sam was not in, but the order was on the ship, I rang back the store and ditto, it was on the ship, with the only proviso being that they were unsure of freezer space.

Okay, we'll run with that.

* * *

Andrew and Raymond have been making incredible progress. The port engine is now going, and they have ascertained that both legs, gearboxes and props are also fine.

Couldn't believe it! My tears flowed freely. It was all coming together at the right time, and just maybe, just maybe, we were going to resurrect our dream.

* * *

Friday came and went, and we wondered about the ship.

Saturday dawned soggily. That's good; more water in the tanks. But will the ship come? Yep! Saw it from about 5 nautical miles off and stared at it all the way in.

Stevedoring is an amazing sight on Mogmog. The ship anchors offshore about 500 metres, and small boats full of people and goods charge backwards and forwards. All the men line up in the water and form a chain stretching from the small boats up to the surf line. They empty the boats in no time, leaving a pile of boxes to be picked over by the women who, me included, looked like a gaggle of bare-breasted seagulls swooping on chips. Then it's out with every available wheelbarrow, and the villagers lug everything back to their houses. Later, the designated delivery men then bring round the invoices for the goods so you can reconcile what you paid for with what you got.

I stood and watched boatloads of rice being taken off the ship by about 40 men, bag by bag. Toss, catch. Toss, catch. Never missed! The bags were bound for the island store; now I knew how it gets provisioned.

Once all the cargo was off, coconuts started going the other way, back from the island to the ship. Hundreds of them, with maybe 25 coconuts in the air at any one time, with all the men bantering and laughing as they worked. Talk about a team. Again it struck me that something like this would never happen back home.

Back at the house, we opened what felt like our Christmas pressies. The hardware first. Opened the huge heavy bag … and there was the largest block and tackle I have ever seen. No hydraulic jacks at all. Couldn't believe it. Rang Sam, and he very proudly told me that, after he had finished his conversation with me, he had had a meeting with his store mates, and they had decided what we really needed was the block and tackle, rather than the jacks. Would've been bloody handy *last week*! *No bloody use now!* Andrew was sorta happy with the timber. It was green, but it was there.

Now for the groceries. Only six medium boxes; I'd expected more. Hmmm. I opened them and found we had about a third of what we ordered. There was no explanation, but the invoice matched the goods, with the noticeable exception of the vodka. Four bottles had apparently 'evaporated' between Yap and here. And guess what? Not a beer or wine in the order or invoice. It was not processed, and not there.

Now let's get this one thing straight. Andrew and I enjoy a drink or few each day, as most Aussies do, and while it was clearly not earth-shattering not to have any alcohol, it certainly made a difference to the prospect of the following weeks. Our socialising now consisted of us sitting quietly after everyone had left us alone for the night, chatting about the day and our hopes for the following day, having a drink under the palms and stars, in peace, together.

I rang the shop and found they had put an $800 limit on our account. They had neglected to tell us this. And they had decided to work out what we really needed. They dropped the beer and wine and the canned vegies off our order but they did send 40 rolls of toilet paper, so it was clear what they thought we must be full of!

TEN

TITANIA DROPS BY AND WE STEP INTO WONDERLAND

Raymond appears in the door on Monday afternoon. 'There's a ship yacht coming! It's 10 miles north and anchoring here.'

Wow! Where from? Who? Where to?

I went down to where Andrew was working on preparing the boat for the beginning of the timber strips that would form the basis of the strip planking of the hull and told him about the ship yacht. We agreed that, with the wind as it was, we would see them in about five minutes. Our guess wasn't quite right. But soon enough we saw a sloop anchor at the next island, named Sorelai, right about where we had drifted from. We got on the VHF and someone named Gina responded from SY *Titania*.

'Bloody hell, she sounds Australian!' I said to Andrew.

Yes, she was! They (whoever they were) had come from Guam and were off to Palau. They planned to come over to Mogmog the following day. Would we like to come aboard for lunch? 'Fantastic!' was our reply.

It was hard to knuckle down for the rest of the day.

* * *

One of the frustrations of life on Mogmog, I had been finding, are the restrictions on what us girls are permitted to do. Because we are not allowed to sweat, literally, we are forbidden from exercising or doing manual work of any kind. (They seem to make an exception for lifting the extremely heavy water bucket out of the well, mind you, or dragging forlorn catamarans up the beach!)

It is also forbidden for women to show their thighs; consequently women go to bed after the men are asleep and rise before they wake so there is no chance of any wardrobe malfunctions being noticed during sleep. The lavalavas are worn all the time, including in bed, and to wash in the ocean. Beats me how they have a population here at all. I have worn them on occasion and, while they are comfortable, you can only sit a couple of ways in them without sacrilegiously baring the thighs! And forget swimming in them; it just doesn't work.

The biggest problem with this male/female division is that I can't help on the boat. I find this incredibly hard. I am supposed to be at home, cooking, washing, looking after kids etc. That's all fine, but where I come from, those duties take up about a third of the day. There's a whole working day in there as well. And my weekends have always been full of doing whatever Andrew is doing, which might be painting, building, lugging or other physical stuff. I'm not a 'sit back and watch them all work' girl. I want to get in there with the fibreglass or sanding.

Despite how much I had to grit my teeth about the ways of Mogmogians, I wasn't about to buck the system. So it was back to the schoolwork with the girls for the rest of the day.

* * *

Next morning, *Titania* anchored off Mogmog. She is a lovely 60-foot sloop, beautifully decked out. Her owners, Richard and Cathy, hail from the United Kingdom but work and live in Korea. They have two children, Oliver and Annie, who are 12 and 10 respectively. The family makes the most of the free time they have. They have a crew who get the boat to their required destination, then Richard and the family meet up with them and do really exciting sailing. What a great lifestyle!

We met Richard, the two kids and the skipper on the beach. Diminutive, blonde Gina is the skipper. She's Tasmanian and a down-to-earth girl with a big smile. She's the sort of girl you immediately like. They were on their way to meet Juanito. Gina was wearing very practical shorts. Oh, my God! Thighs!

'Stay right there, Gina! I'll get you a sarong.'

This crisis averted, we escorted the visitors to Juanito's place then showed them around 'our' island.

Oliver wanted to see the store, which is on the other side of the island, the bit I think of as the back of the island, so I took him there. It's a simple wooden house with a tin roof; the nearby shed belongs to it, too. Inside there is no lighting. That day, the wooden shelves held about six cans of tuna, six cans of sardines, assorted toiletries, batteries, a heap of carnation milk tins and, in the corner, a big stack of noodle boxes. The sort that you boil for two minutes. At home they are called two-minute noodles. Andrew has always told the kids they are called that because you have to eat them in two minutes.

Oliver's eyes were bugging out of his head. 'That's the shop? That's it?'

'Yup, that's it.'

'For the whole island?'

'Yup, for the whole island.'

Next we showed everyone through our salubrious accommodation. Gina's reaction was, 'Hey, you've got a roof, toilet, water and power. Bloody good start.' (Told you I liked her!)

'I don't know,' said Oliver.

We introduced the kids to jacks, aka knucklebones, played around here with rocks, and then they invited us back to the boat.

Oh, frabjous day!

There we met Cathy; Kate, the amazing chef; and the rest of the crew. They are all of the same ilk as Gina. All thoroughly great!

Richard and Cathy made us feel so welcome. They set up the

kids downstairs with piles of food and cold drinks. Oliver had made dessert. It was a masterpiece of Oreos, Gingernuts and cream all mooshed together in a sweet, crunchy and soft pile. Wonderful!

For the adults up on deck, Kate produced a lunch consisting of a cold-meat platter, no less than eight different cheeses, couscous salad, Caesar salad, fruit salad, a cracker selection and hot herb bread, served with whatever you liked to drink. Andrew looked like he'd died and gone to heaven as he was presented with an icy Corona with lime. My slice of heaven was a great, cold, crisp white wine. Does it get any better?

We ate our hosts out of house and home, and had a wonderful afternoon with them all. Fabulous company. Lots of laughs. It's difficult to describe how it all felt. I guess it was a bit like Alice falling down the hole.

At about 4 o'clock we had to make our goodbyes because they were off to Yap. As we left they gave us a bottle of vodka, a bottle of wine, apples, oranges and lollies, a book on cruising and 4 litres of epoxy resin. Fantastic!

Titania moved out of sight and we waved a sad goodbye. The whole visit had been like a bolt out of the blue. Had it all really happened?

It had been real, and *Titania* had left a legacy that outlasted the goodies. During the course of the afternoon, Richard talked me into writing this book. So it's all his fault, really.

Also, we had described — or is that moaned about? — our experiences ordering provisions, particularly alcohol. As we kicked around ideas, someone had the thought of getting Amos, the pilot from Pacific Missionary Aviation, to fly some out to us. He flies out from Yap each Monday and Friday, bringing passengers and limited supplies, such as betel nut and rice. This effectively is Mogmog's only constant contact with the 'real world'. We were told Amos couldn't fly out 'adult beverages' as it's a missionary plane, and the missionary charter and alcohol do not mix. He had, however, offered to bring us anything else we need.

Aha! There's the answer.

* * *

Next morning, we received an email from Gina. At Yap she had purchased some 'distilled water' for us and had left it at the police station for the pilot to bring on Friday. Gotta love ingenuity! They had bought and used the water for themselves, then bought 5 litres of vodka and filled the distilled water bottle with vodka, and there you go! No one's the wiser!

Come Friday, Andrew and I went the 5 nautical miles to Falalop in the dinghy. Very wet trip! Once there, among other things, we waited for the plane. It duly arrived and we met Amos, a tall, sandy-haired man with a big friendly smile. He came over, warmly introduced himself and handed us a 5-litre bottle of 'distilled water'.

Unknown to us at the time, Amos was to become a large part of our lives on Mogmog. A very welcome part.

We love you, *Titania*!

And good luck in the Sydney to Hobart race this year!

ELEVEN

SOME INTRICACIES OF MOGMOG LIFE

Did you know that lime trees are bad luck? No one on Mogmog ever lives near lime trees. Not sure which came first, the houses or the lime trees, but the houses near the lime trees are empty because of the bad luck.

Also, have you been feeling off-colour at all lately? Maybe you walked past a pumpkin vine that was about to flower. That'll do it every time, you know. It's how you know your pumpkin's about to flower.

Here's a handy one. If you have done something and want to hide your actions from a particular individual, it's easy! All you need to do is put a cloth or a towel over your head and walk around like that for the whole day. You can go wherever you want — though you'll tend to sit by yourself — and you may talk to whomever you please, but the person you are hiding from cannot come and talk to you. You may continue this as long as you wish. Perfect!

Now a word or two on sleeping. Sigh. Our 'bedroom' has two louvre windows, one either side of the mattress on the floor. On the adjacent wall, there is a hinged window, one side of which is permanently jammed shut. We picked that spot in the hope we would get some breeze through; the nights here are hot and can be very still, so you end up soaked in sweat.

Bear with me while I describe more about our set-up. There are three main streets on the island that come together in a Y, right about where we are living. Some genius in years gone by decided it would be a good idea to pave the three streets with coral. This has the advantage of keeping sand down, and mud out of houses, so I guess that is why they did it. But it also has the effect of being impossible to walk on without thongs, and you go through a pair of them every three weeks walking on this stuff. But the thing about coral is that it's also very noisy to walk on, and we can hear people coming and going for about 200 metres. When the houses get too hot, people take their bedrolls or sleeping mats and go down to the beach — they traipse right past our windows.

The houses here are all quite close together, and the emphasis is very much on a family lifestyle. So I can tell you which babies have trouble sleeping, who has a cold, and who needed to go to the loo when. Most loo visits involve a trip to the beach — and a walk past our window!

The neighbourhood dogs deserve a big mention. Currently we

have seven puppies within 50 metres of the house, and there is no better time for a puppy rumble than between 12 and 2am, and the more puppies the better. Then we have Rolande next door, who is a gorgeous dog with the unfortunate habit of yipping constantly every otherish night for an hour or so. Her owners don't seem to hear it, but then they are probably exhausted, as they have one of those babies that doesn't sleep, plus an autistic boy who often wakes upset in the middle of the night.

Add to this racket the odd coconut or breadfruit landing on the tin roof and bouncing all the way to the ground, where it lands with a thud.

To top things off, we have the roosters. They are all good mates, these roosters, so when you hear one rooster crowing about something in the distance, his close mates will make sure that all the other roosters on the island know about it. The crowing comes like a Mexican wave from afar, with the sound crescendoing up to you and then receding into the distance.

Of course the main reason for this is to let the other roosters know it's morning. This is where the roosters are a bit challenged. If you think like a rooster, every time a cloud covers the moon, it's obviously night time. So just as obviously, when the moon comes out, it must be morning. Consequently we have about 40 nights and mornings for each rooster each night. I reckon KFC need to set up here!

Then like clockwork, a gentle breeze wafts through the house at about 5am, and all is calm, and with profound relief we drop off to sleep.

CLANG CLANG CLANG
CLANG CLANG CLANG
CLANG CLANG CLANG
CLANG CLANG CLANG
CLANG CLANG CLANG CLANG CLANG CLANG
CLANG CLANG CLANG

CLANG

That's 6am; the pattern never varies. We roll over in disbelief. A minute later, we're asleep.

CLANG CLANG CLANG
CLANG CLANG CLANG
CLANG CLANG CLANG
CLANG CLANG CLANG
CLANG CLANG CLANG CLANG CLANG CLANG
CLANG CLANG CLANG
CLANG CLANG

Oh, no. It's 6.30. At that, we struggle up off the mattress and head for the cold-water spout in the bathroom.

By the time the 'get up you lazy bastards' bell clangs at 6.50, Andrew and I are sitting under a frangipani tree with a cuppa, feeling like we've both been run over by a truck.

This is an everyday occurrence.

While at our coffee spot, a succession of small kids come up for what has become a daily ritual. Three-year-old Keira is always first. Behind her are shy Renae and older Raelene.

'Monmai lemailion.' [Good morning.]

'Monmai lemailion, Keira.'

'Sihatfa?' [How are you?]

'Tifarachoh.' [Very well.]

'Sihatfa?'

'Tifarachoh.'

'Langah.' [See you.]

'Langah, Keira.'

Then it would be Renae's turn, and then Raelene, and so on.

The kids have a real problem saying Andrew, so they came up with Andirew, with the emphasis on the i, so there's a chorus of 'Langah, Andirew' whenever he walks past. Hilarious.

In the evenings we often wander through the village to say hi to Juanito. It's a walk lined with vivid, multicoloured frangipanis, which perfume the entire village. Many of these trees are filled with chickens that roost in the boughs. I've never looked up into a tree to see a chicken before. Pigs are attached to palm trees at each house and occasionally we see enormous coconut crabs strung from the trees for safekeeping, like giant alien Christmas baubles.

As we walk we are greeted by all the dogs on our route, culminating with KK and Nikon, Juanito's pooches. Along the way, the 'Langahs' of daytime are replaced with 'Sabongs' (Good nights), like a chorus from each house.

TWELVE

WE MAKE GIANT STRIDES

An amazing thing happened. The other day, four boys aged about 10 or 11 struggled, dripping wet, up the beach to us carrying what looked like — but couldn't possibly be, could it? — our anchor. It was!

These boys had taken it upon themselves to swim out maybe 700 metres with an inflatable ring, dive till they found the anchor, haul it up (no mean feat!), and get it and its 70 metres of chain back to the shore. Although I've never weighed the thing, I know I can't lift it without huge heaps of oomph, and that's with no chain. How they did it I'll never know! When I tried to thank them, they went all bashful and disappeared. What an effort. I hope they know just how appreciated it was.

Now we had one of the two anchors back. Phew!

* * *

We had discovered from Raymond, who is the HF and VHF operator for the island, and therefore is the information centre, that the supply ship turn-around at Yap was going to be shorter than usual this time, and the ship would be back probably the coming Thursday. That meant only two weeks since the last ship.

We were determined to get the ordering process right this time. I rang Amos, and asked if I could fly out with him to Yap on the Monday, with a view to doing all our shopping — ensuring there were no slip-ups — and then sitting with our stuff to babysit it safely back 'home'. Amos had no problem with that. Great!

Amos had already offered to let us use his address as a 'meeting place' for everything coming to us from all over the world. He would then fly it out to us, as he could, weight and space permitting. He offered to take our very misshapen rudder to Yap and to despatch it to Palau, where Dennis was waiting to catch it. Bless *his* cotton socks! And this was free of charge! He offered to get anything we needed, whenever, and gave his personal email address to help. He even offered to slightly bend the rules of what he could and couldn't transport by air, so that we didn't have to wait for the ship. Amos for *emperor*!

Next hurdle: let's pay the Yap Co-operative account. They don't take credit cards over the phone — or any other way for that matter. This I already knew. Okay, plan B: get to Falalop to use the internet (they have wifi there, can you believe that?), so that

I could EFT funds to their account. I rang them to get account details. Remember the earlier phone conversations when I tracked down Ali, trying to set up the account? I won't repeat the whole painstaking drama; just take it as being exactly the same.

The people at the Yap Co-operative had never heard of EFT, so I explained it to them, and eventually got an account number. No chance of a BSB, though. No amount of explaining was going to work for that.

In desperation, I rang the bank in Yap and asked if the account number I had been given was one of theirs; I was assured that it was. I then asked for the BSB and was greeted with silence. When I explained to the person on the other end of the phone that it was a bank branch identifier, she cheerfully said, 'Oh yes! We are number three.' Somehow, I didn't think that was going to work.

Soon I realised that 'Duh, dear idiot', an EFT wasn't going to work anyway as I wasn't going to be putting the money into an Australian bank. I would have to do an international transfer. That actually made it easier because, if memory served correctly, you didn't need a BSB for those.

We checked with Raymond that the internet in Falalop was up and running. No problem, we were assured. Next day, Andrew and I made another soggy trip there in the dinghy. This dinghy is the bane of our lives. It has a laminated fibreglass hull with inflatable pontoons. It is only two years old, but in that time the hull has delaminated so that it has filled with water, making it hugely heavy and difficult to haul around. Also, the glue in the seams of the pontoons has deteriorated to the point that air leaks out the gaps. As soon as we fix one part of the seam, the next blows out, so that now nearly all the seam is a series of patches, that themselves fail over time. Thus a trip to Falalop for two, means that while one person is driving, the other alternates between pumping up the pontoons and pumping out the water that swamps us every time a wave gets us. As the dinghy deflates, the waves become more effective at swamping you.

On arrival, we were informed that the internet was down indefinitely. Great! So then we made contact with Amos, only to be told that he couldn't fit me in the plane on Monday after all. There was a funeral on the island, and all seats were taken. Okay, no internet, no plane on Monday. Control freaks — don't apply for this one!

Determined to achieve something from the trip, we introduced ourselves to Mario, Raymond's brother-in-law and boss, who runs the power on Falalop and its outer islands. After we paid to have more power at our abode, we got chatting and told him about our various problems buying supplies from the Yap Co-operative and getting them delivered. Immediately he came up with a solution to the theft issue. Our order from Yap, he said, could be stored in the hold along with his order for his store. Apparently one of his brothers worked at the co-op, and if I could let the co-op know, his brother would ensure that our goods did actually get into the hold. That cheered us up.

At our next stop, we were able to buy some Sprite to go with our new 'distilled water'. The day was picking up.

On the way back, I realised that maybe Suzzanne, Andrew's sister, might be able to be our banker. As soon as I got home, I emailed her our bank details, including passwords, and she cheerfully said she'd take care of it! Bless her cotton socks!

But we weren't yet out of the woods. Next morning, Sue emailed me with bad news. Our bank had no reciprocal arrangement with the Bank of the Federated States of Micronesia or any other Micronesian banking institution for that matter. She had tried her bank, thinking we could pay her back, and run into a brick wall there, too. A credit-card cash advance hadn't worked. She'd even rung two banks' helplines on a Saturday: no luck. Clearly she has the patience of a saint! Full marks for trying, Sue!

Somewhere in her email, however, was a mention of Western Union, the global money transfer company. Another 'duh' moment! Of course!

Straight away I rang my mother and explained our predicament. Mum — in typical Mum style — took everything down very carefully — *very* carefully — and then did exactly what we asked, saying to forget paying her back till we get things sorted. Bless *her* cotton socks! She also sent some money to Amos, who had agreed to act as a kind of banker. Of the funds she transferred, he would give us half in cash and keep the rest in a kitty for us. In the future, we would let him know what we needed and he would take the necessary money out of kitty.

With cash now about to flow and safe goods transport worked out, there only remained the order to be placed. Although we had had technical problems with our email, it was working again so I abandoned the sat phone and went with email instead. The shopping list went on forever, but it was soooo much easier this time.

Once again it felt like Christmas Eve, mostly because we didn't know if we would actually get what we wanted. When I rang to confirm the email order, I was told by the store that they had had to make substitutes, but that it was basically all there, including Andrew's carton of beer. This last fact was proudly stated.

* * *

'Did you say carton?'

'Yes, one carton.'

'Oh, no. It was 13 cartons, not one.'

'Thirteen?'

'Yes, 13. And 12 flagons of wine.'

'Yes, we have the 12 bottles of wine.'

'Three-litre flagons?'

'No, 12 bottles.'

Oh, crumbs. That would test our savoir faire!

After some painstaking negotiation with the incredulous person on the other end of the phone, I got acknowledgment of our order, and his proclamation that everything was in stock. Phew.

Next I rang the hardware store and was proudly told that Sam had a day off today, but they had got everything onto the boat by themselves!

Oh, dear. Hold onto your hats, Barries! Juanito had given us the go-ahead to paint our living quarters so I had asked for paint, as well as for prices on brushes and rollers, as they can vary so much. No word on that; Christmas Eve again! Also I had asked for paint colours and no answer was forthcoming. Oh, well. Time would tell.

* * *

Boy, have you guys been busy! Main thing is that you are all together and safe and nobody was hurt. That is some kind of adventure that you have had. Hope you are getting lots of footage for a book or National Geographic.

You are very brave to stay … but there again, everyone knows that Andrew could probably fix the boat with a roll of sticky tape!

Hoping it goes your way.

The Simos

* * *

Things were moving right along with repairing *Windrider*. Andrew wanted a frame to stand at the back of the boat to support it while it was being jacked so he had made a sort of H-shaped one out of a huge tree trunk and pine timber. It had to support 8 tons, so needed to be dug about 4 feet into the sand. Eight men lifted it into place.

Assembling the frame took about four days; the support had to be hand-sawn and the logs had to be found around the island then hauled to the spot. Big job.

He too was losing his savoir faire. As long as I've known Andrew, about 100 years, he has suffered physically when he's suffered emotionally. It's just a matter of when. He had been battling coral-cut infections and had resorted to taking a course of antibiotics, plus he was trying not to get the flu, when he got a ripper stomach bug.

I got out of bed when I heard him calling from the bathroom. He was about to faint while on the throne, and was on the verge of throwing up as well as needing to be on the toilet. I scrambled to get damp towels and a bowl, and we had one of those 'for better or for worse' moments. Slowly the feeling passed. He was a mess for the rest of the night and couldn't move next morning. This was, naturally, when the ship came in.

Originally, the arrangement was that our groceries would come to Falalop with Mario's order and the hardware to Mogmog. Mario radioed Raymond and suggested that, seeing as the ship had stopped at Mogmog first, we might as well get everything off here, and he would backstop anything at Falalop that slipped through the cracks. Good thought!

So Raymond came by wanting Andrew to come out to the ship, go down into the hold, ID our order, and stay with it until it arrived at shore.

That was just not going to happen. When I said I'd do it, he looked a bit startled but agreed. So I slipped out of the lavalava and into long shorts then headed out into the surf, into the boat — soaking wet — and out to the ship. Climbed up the side of the ship and climbed the ladder down into the hold. It felt great! Finally, I was doing something physical. Raymond seemed bemused. He stood watching me, with his hands on his hips, head to one side, eyes practically grinning, while a small smile played across the rest of his face. Our dry goods were easy to find, and I spotted most of the frozen foods quickly enough. Mario later found two boxes that I missed. Yay for him! It all got ashore safely, albeit wetly, and so did I.

This time, there was a whole lot more to unpack than before, and all the village kids were hanging around our place so I shooed them out before starting. At this stage, we'd already seen enough of our stuff going to the benefit of others, and the next ship was about eight weeks away. I was determined to keep a tight rein on provisions.

After going through the paperwork, we were chuffed; we had received exactly what the people at the co-op said they had sent us. No parcels had gone missing. Thanks, Mario!

The next thing was to open the parcels and see what they had actually given us. There were hinges for the house windows, but no screws; paint but no paint brushes or rollers; and 18 containers of pudding and jelly instead of canned vegies. A few things were not there at all. But, hey, it wasn't bad!

Once Andrew had spent all of Thursday resting, he perked up a lot. On the Friday, it was back to Falalop to meet Amos, who greeted us with his now familiar grin, $500 in an envelope and three large bags of betel nut for Juanito. Then we were able to watch the damaged rudder being flown away to Palau. Half its luck!

Another bite of the elephant.

THIRTEEN

CALAMITY STRIKES

'Quick, Jen. Where's the morphine?'

'In the safe in the boat! I'll get it. Who? What?'

'Crushed hand.'

And he was gone.

I raced to the boat, which had been raised about 5 feet off the sand, and somehow climbed up; made it, just. Grabbed morphine tablets and frozen peas, and raced back to who knew where, or to whom.

Turns out, Glen and Keith, two young men, had been helping Andrew to jack the boat up from the solid timber frame he had made. They'd been jacking it up inch by inch, then pausing and placing pieces of wood into the gaps made, little by little bringing the boat to a more workable height. Glen had been putting a piece of wood into a gap when the new jack gave way. Instantly, 8 tons of boat fell on his hand, pinning it to a timber stack.

Glen, in agony, had kept saying, 'Please, please, Andrew, you have to help me. Please, please get the boat off my hand!'

He had Andrew's full attention!

The jack was useless where it was. The boat had slid sideways, so that the timber that had been under and supporting the jack was no longer under the hull of the boat. Now there was only coral and beach sand under the hull, which offered no support for a jack. Because the timber support was dug 4 feet into the sand, it couldn't be moved, and there was no chance of finding other timber quickly. Andrew decided to put the jack on an angle from the timber support to the boat hull. It was still functional. Being hydraulic, it had been overloaded and had come down unexpectedly, but luckily was still usable. It was pretty risky, which he wasn't happy about, but there was no quick alternative.

Fortunately, the angled jack worked and the boat was lifted enough for Glen to remove his hand. Later on, Andrew told me that if it hadn't worked, he'd have had to amputate Glen's fingers to free him. Or, worse, he'd had visions of the boat sliding off the wooden supports and crushing Glen, who would have had no way to extricate himself while his hand was pinned.

The sight of the freed hand, Andrew said, was physically sickening. The fingers were about 2mm thick. That is not even the depth of the bones! Through all this, Glen maintained his composure, and he kept expressing his gratitude.

That bit was awful. Andrew and I both felt a huge sense of responsibility. Glen had been helping us, and it was our boat that had fallen on him. Okay, what were his hands doing right between the boat and the frame? But there's not much point debating that after the event, is there?

By the time I arrived on the scene, Glen was surrounded by people intent on helping. He had been taken to our neighbour's house, as he had been related to the now deceased traditional medicine expert. I had little idea of their level of first-aid or medical knowledge, and was conscious of that fine line: between helping and upsetting some local guru. But when they put Glen's hand into a bowl of leaves and hot water, I couldn't sit back. I sent the girls to find the icepacks while I wrapped his hand with frozen peas. Andrew had already raced off to Raymond's house, where Mogmog's VHF radio is kept, to get info on if or where a doctor might be available.

After I gave Glen 5mg of morphine, I had a look at the hand. There was extensive bruising, but little in the way of laceration. I touched the pads of his fingers and they all had feeling. Phew!

Having convinced the gathering that ice was the way to go, rather than hot water, I climbed back onto the boat and rang the Royal Flying Doctor Service in Jandakot, Western Australia. A professional mariner mate had told me that they have a doctor on standby, and they will help you over the phone wherever you are. He was right. Thanks, John!

It took a while to establish some kind of useful dialogue

because they couldn't work out why this woman was ringing from a remote island in the Pacific:

'Madam, you have actually rung a place called Jandakot in Perth, Australia.'

'Bloody glad to hear that! Now can I speak to a doctor, *please*?!'

'I think you should be going through the Eastern States for this, madam.'

'But why? No one is going to come out here, so what difference does the other side of the country make to telephone advice?'

After several minutes of that hoo ha, I was put on to a very helpful doctor. His initial recommendation was to get Glen to an x-ray and post-trauma management facility. Ummmm, not going to happen.

He had me indent Glen's nails to check for circulation. All fine! I was amazed, happy and extremely relieved. Glen would not lose his fingers. Multiple fractures were inevitable, but being a veteran of a number of broken fingers, I knew that treatment is basically nil anyway.

The doctor and I discussed pain management, and fortunately Andrew and I had everything he suggested in our first-aid kit. It was a minor miracle because we had had a lot of trouble obtaining morphine for the trip. I went to three doctors before managing to convince one to prescribe it for me. The doctor had to phone the pharmacist and give an explanation before he could hand over the script. Then the pharmacist had to order it in specially. What a rigmarole! Even getting Panadeine Forte had been tricky.

Motivated by visions of being stuck somewhere in a dire medical situation, I had persevered. Glad I did. I really don't understand the issue here. Morphine is hardly a party drug.

It was obvious when the pain medication kicked in because Glen started to joke, which was great to see. He reckoned he was the star of the day. Andrew asked him not to lend a hand again.

Raymond managed to make radio contact with a medic in Falalop. He was as close to a doctor as it comes here. He had known the Western doctor, who had subsequently died, and had learned from him. His name was also Andrew, and he agreed to come over immediately. Thirteen wet miles by dinghy.

He turned out to be a nice guy, and agreed with the advice of the RFDS doctor. He put Glen on a precautionary course of antibiotics, and gave him some lower-dosage painkillers.

During the afternoon and evening, we wandered past Glen's place a few times, and he was in good spirits. Made of tough stuff that boy!

This all happened only yesterday. This morning Glen came over to our place and said, 'I wanted to show you this.' And he unwrapped his hand and held it out to me. 'Look. All better!'

And, bugger me, all the swelling was gone, as was the bruising. It looked as if it was back to normal. I couldn't believe my eyes! I asked him to clench his fist, and he tried but was immediately in a whole heap of obvious pain. Hmmm, that will be the fractures.

That hand will be sore for some weeks, but then it will be a functioning hand with all its fingers. And I'm betting there'll be no repeat of that accident.

By the way, we discovered that Glen's family can't afford power to their house. We fixed that. Some things are way easier to fix than others.

FOURTEEN

THE STATE OF AFFAIRS AFTER ONE MONTH

No, No, No ... You want adventure on the high *seas*. Not adventure on the high *reefs*! Do they get everything backward in Australia?

I am just re-reading your email from April 21 and am amazed at what you are getting done there. It is truly an adventure and you are getting an experience few others will. I know, the price in anxiety and even danger has been high. But look at the rewards. The girls will remember this for the rest of their long lives as a Robinson Crusoe experience. You may have wrecked them for a 'normal' life. They will spend the rest of their years trying to recreate the past two. Good on them if they are successful!

Bill and Amy

Current Position

N02 00 E108 01

We have now been here a month. Time to take stock. There are plenty of positives to reflect on.

We are now accepted members of a new community. Along the way, we have made serious faux pas that we have been told about. Hope there aren't too many we haven't known of.

Last night I put my foot in it. Around here, there is no word for hello. The closest they have is 'Would you like to come and eat?' The correct answer to this is 'Thank you, I've eaten', or 'Thank you, I'm full.' When the kids and I were passing Stanley's house, he loudly invited us in, so I accepted. He was chatting to a friend, Francis, and he invited me to join them and have a tuba. I did, but shouldn't have; Francis politely made to leave, and I realised it was because of me. Oops. He had come all the way from Falalop to see Stanley, and I felt bad to have messed up the visit, not that it was on purpose.

Another mistake was Andrew wearing a towel as a thu. Bad move. Towels are associated with ablutions and not to be worn outside the bathroom.

Shan unknowingly did the wrong thing by wearing a lavalava. Lavalavas are only to be worn from when you first have a period. All the other kids were complaining that they weren't allowed to wear them, so why could she?

Leaving all that aside, I think and hope the people of Mogmog like us.

We have become the local Bunnings store, and Juanito uses us as his corner store. I think it's to pay the rent where we are living.

Any order we get in from Yap includes beer, vodka, cigarettes and other sundries for Juanito's place.

The boat is starting to take shape. Just yesterday, Andrew started sanding back the area where he will start the timber repair structure. Suddenly it looks like any one of his projects, rather than a disaster.

We have established supply lines we think will work. If a friend in need is a pain in the arse, boy are we giant pains in the arse at the moment! Paul Walker, our great mate, who lives around the corner from us in Perth, has been wonderful. He is an internet junkie who has the sometimes infuriating habit of deliberating through something from more angles than you would've believed possible, and he has been using these skills to help us track down parts. To have achieved what he has, he has to have been working almost full-time on our hassles.

He has sourced the two inverters we need — one local, one overseas — and they are either being delivered to him or directly to us. Also, Paul has established a super-helpful contact in Guam named Randy, who is taking it on himself to organise all things fibreglass and resin; that's a big list! Paul has coordinated with Randy for us, bearing in mind we have only recently got our email running again. He has lined up pumps and myriad other bits and pieces for us.

Yanmar Australia, the marine diesel engine people, have been fantastic. The parts we need are only superficial, but they come to $6000. Believe me, getting shipwrecked is not a cheap pastime. They have agreed to give us the parts and get them to us free of charge, in exchange for a few testimonials and photos. Talk about a fantastic product with fantastic support. Our Palauan friends have also been wanting to help. Dennis is ringing us regularly and doing heaps on our behalf there in Palau. He is waiting for Amos to deliver the rudder and is going to either repair the existing stainless steel frame, or fabricate a new one. Jay is providing weather information. Sam is allowing us to use his operation as a delivery and forwarding address in Palau. Mum is solving cash logistics for us; ATMs are hard to come by in Micronesia, and this region does not use credit cards at all. Consequently, Mum and Western Union have become good friends. I'm going to owe her a fortune!

Andrew's sister, Sue, is our banker, and is dispersing more funds than I want to know about from our accounts.

My sister, Lindy, is sending us books, sunglasses (the glare here is amazing) and, more importantly, chocolate. Paul and Fee have burnt off 35 movies and bought umpteen DVDs so we retain our night-time sanity.

And we have learned of heaps of friends who have sent packages to us and the girls. We haven't received any yet, but just to know that people have done that for us is an amazing feeling.

Once we got email back up two weeks ago, I realised just how much I missed everyone at home, and the day-to-day contact we have with them.

Also what staggered me is that our Palauan friends, although new, are by no stretch of the imagination fair-weather friends. It was Jay who knew where we were when the typhoon struck, and

Jay who was on the email all that night, attempting to maintain contact. The emails we have received from home and Palau have had me in tears regularly, both of laughter and sadness. I miss you all, you scaly bunch. And my new Darwinian mate, Louise. Well, you have to read her emails to understand.

* * *

Day-to-day life has settled into a pattern. The bell clangs us awake at 6am. Andrew and I have a cuppa, and then he heads to the boat. The girls and I settle into schoolwork at about 8.30. Schoolwork provides sanity and regularity. We considered sending them to school here, but the principal didn't think it would work out well for our girls as they are fairly significantly ahead, and chats with Deb, their wonderful School of Isolated and Distance Education (SIDE) teacher, convinced me they are better with the SIDE program. It is a great program — and Deb, you're a gem!

We spread out our cooking, using the microwave, which miraculously still works, the gas barbeque from the boat and a single burner gas ring that Andrew, who is nothing if not determined, had had me biking around five stores in Palau to find. That might not sound so bad, but Koror, the main island of Palau, is a long island with a huge spinelike ridge running along it. So every time you go to another hardware or department store, it means going up or down the ribs, and up a bit more spine, and then down and up another rib and back to the spine. All this in

80ish per cent humidity. You try it! And all of this for an item that we *might* use camping occasionally. Now, I'm very glad he did!

So with those we're fine. Diet is a bit tricky. Fruit and veg consist of breadfruit, bananas, taro and papaya (not in season), plus the odd pumpkin, hence the need for canned vegies, not *jelly*! Papayas are eaten green, when they are cooked as a vegetable. Ripe, they are treated as a fruit. Also, all the fruit trees and taro are privately owned, so we don't have access to anything, unless someone gives it to us. If you help yourself to anything from the island or the sea, you are stealing.

The freezer on the boat is running again, thanks to Andrew's repairs, but we have no refrigeration at the house, so organising our perishables is a bit of a juggle. If the ship has been and we have fresh fruit and vegies, we have to eat them as quickly as possible as the humidity just destroys them within days. Apples and oranges are much better and will last up to four weeks. Potatoes last about two weeks before becoming moosh. Pumpkins are fantastic and will last indefinitely, as long as they are uncut. Other than the pumpkins, I can eke fruit and veg out for four to six weeks.

Dishes are washed in our crayfish cooking pot at the back of the house, and the dirty water is put on my new pumpkin plants.

Clothes washing is done at the well, which has guppies in it to combat mozzies, and is done as infrequently as possible. It's really quite hard work doing the laundry with a scrubbing brush. Fortunately, the lack of tops reduces the washing a lot.

The well is about five houses away from where we are living. It borders on the ancient taro patch at the back of the island. It is surrounded by bananas and papayas and is a raised concrete square that sits 2 feet above the ground and then continues down approximately 15 feet to the natural fresh water lens under the island. To get the water there are two buckets, made from fishing buoys, and these have to be hauled up the 15 feet. I dropped one in the well on Day 1. In terms of Mogmog etiquette, that has to be the worst thing in the world to do.

Embarrassedly, I went and explained to Andrew what had happened. He was very understanding and told me the locals would now probably eat me! So I found a long pole with a hook — used for cutting down coconuts — and sheepishly fished out the bucket, with Andrew offering heaps of supportive advice … *not*. There were a number of sniggers as I passed various houses carrying the long pole I had found.

A dunny brush and dunny cleaner arrived with the last ship, and that was a fantastic day. Before that the toilet was putridly horrible, with stains from God knows when. It made such a difference to be able to go to a clean loo!

All food scraps go to the multitude of pigs around the place. Mogmog has puppies bursting out of its seams. Unfortunately, some of these end up being dinner. Not much I can do about that. But I am trying to change the way dogs are treated. Juanito has said to me a number of times that he can't believe that all the dogs like me. The dogs here are skittish and timid, something to do with constantly being kicked and having stones thrown at them. I am trying to show the people here, and it's starting to work, that treating a dog as a pet and friend can make a huge difference.

FIFTEEN

PARADISE LOST AND FOUND

'Quick, Jen. Wake up!'

'Gees, what now? I just got to sleep.'

'We need sutures and steri strips now!'

'Why? Who?' A sense of déjà vu passed through me.

So restarted the worst night of our idyllic island-retreat holiday, a night that reshaped how I think about the people of Mogmog in a number of ways.

I stepped outside the house. Guys were yelling and running in the dark. It was very hard to work out what was going on. Then I noticed that Mike was on the ground holding his head, blood everywhere. Mike is Alberta's son, and one of the men she had warned us against. He lives a few doors from us, and is a pretty quiet guy who we knew only fleetingly. He has a reputation for heavy drinking, and a temper that flares quickly. Four big guys surrounded him, yelling while they applied a leaf concoction to the gash in his head. It was obvious to me that the wound was serious and needed stitching; we had everything required to do that. I tried to get Mike to come with me to the house, where there was at least light, so we could work out the extent of the damage. He quietened a little, and then let out a hellish shriek and bolted off, shouting that he was going for Raymond.

What next? None of this was making any sense yet. We got to Raymond's in time to see Antoinette, his lovely 13-year-old daughter, screaming hysterically, being dragged along the ground by her hair by a man I hadn't seen before. Jolene, Raymond's wife, was nearby, screeching and flying at Mike. That didn't look like a good plan to me. A very tense Raymond was pacing, but not looking like he was going to help Antoinette or Jolene.

I flew at the guy dragging Antoinette and screamed at him to stop, telling him that if he ever, ever, ever treated a woman like that again, I was going to … I don't know, really; he was 20ish and huge, so I have no idea what I was thinking. But he looked bloody surprised and let her go. Women simply don't assert themselves on Mogmog, so my outburst must have shocked him into submission.

Antoinette was a shaking, hysterical mess and her sobbing verged on screaming. I just hugged her for what seemed like ages, but was probably about 30 minutes.

During this 30 minutes I learned (not from Antoinette) that Mike had been on the tuba for a long while — nothing unusual there! — and had got himself into an argument with another man — nothing unusual there — except that this time it erupted into this really ugly mess. The argument had been over Mike's wife, for reasons I still don't know. Somehow Raymond was implicated, so Mike went to his place — where, as usual, there was a group watching TV out the front — and started causing trouble. Raymond then grabbed a dive torch, wrapped it around his hand a few times, and whacked Mike on the head. As well as injuring Mike, this totally enraged him. There was no sense in Mike that night, and very little from anyone else. We never found out why Antoinette was treated that way.

Andrew reappeared from I don't know where; he, too, had been trying to help Mike. After a quick comparing of notes, we decided to keep completely neutral, and only play first-aid officers.

After Antoinette calmed down, things seemed sufficiently stable and we left. We went home very shaken, poured ourselves stiff drinks and just sat feeling vulnerable and shell-shocked. A knock a little while later revealed Raymond, Jolene and Antoinette at our front door. They came in, sat with us and had a drink. Antoinette was quiet and withdrawn, Raymond was unapologetic and Jolene talked a lot but didn't really say anything. Their view was that Mike had it coming to him and that Raymond did the right thing. This was not our assessment at all, but it's not our culture.

After they left, we sat in the dark and quietly talked, trying to make sense of everything that had happened. We had another drink and another and soon it was about 4am. Where had the time gone? We went to bed but didn't sleep properly. In the morning we woke feeling a sense of the unreal and a complete flatness.

On Mogmog there are no police to call when violence erupts, as it does frequently. These men are big and strong; they don't handle tuba well but drink a lot of it.

Andrew and I were in a volatile situation and we knew that we had to tread carefully, so as not to be seen to be doing anything other than helping — and that is helping both sides.

The feelings of loss and emptiness persisted when we went to visit Mike. We dabbed Betadine on his wound and gave him advice about caring for his injuries. He was suffering from significant blurriness and a very sore head — not quite sure how much was because of the blows from the torch and how much was the aftermath of all the tuba.

We kept an eye on him and, despite our best efforts, the wound began to fester so we gave him antibiotics. It didn't get stitches or even steri-stripped. We really tried but he refused.

* * *

Andrew and I wandered down to the boat alone and just sat. No words. Just sat. Chook and Shan were doing schoolwork and happily occupied, so we decided to walk ... and walk. We found ourselves at the end of the island alone, so we perched on the shelving coral and looked at the day.

It was the bluest of days. My eyes hurt. The coral was white, the water was still and clear and shallow. A black-tipped reef shark cruised slowly past. We moved into the water. Then the most amazing thing happened. We kissed, which in itself is not amazing at all, but what it led to was the most wonderful reaffirmation of our love, and the importance and centrality of that love to our lives. The world simply disappeared. It was us — only us.

The passion was unbelievably intense, and kept building, ebbing, building and ebbing. Time really can stop. The world really can stop. It was the two of us alone in the world on that deserted beach, where we melded physicality with the emotion that has held us together for over 30 years. Reality was what we made it together. We have always enjoyed an intense physical relationship that has our friends shaking their heads, but this was different. I will never forget the look in Andrew's eyes, the depth of emotion, the depth of soul in those eyes for hour upon magical hour.

That increased level of intimacy was not something that had been missing in any way, yet it has lifted us, given an increased sense of what we can do together.

We'll get out of here, and we'll be stronger together for it. Even though this is a much bigger test than the typhoon ever was.

* * *

A couple of days passed and we had an extraordinary night; this one was good extraordinary.

You know, when we arrived here, we thought boredom was going to be a problem. Forget it! We haven't watched DVDs in nights, and every time we try to get a bit of time to ourselves, it's another 'forget it'!

This 'forget it' began with Andrew and I sitting outside in the dark silence, beneath a clouded full moon, listening to the wind in the palms. It was a nice moment that didn't last.

We were joined by a guy who was hoping to intercept his illicit lover on her way back from the farewell dinner her family had prepared; she was about to go back to her husband in Guam. Our guest raced off into the night in hot pursuit of his lady.

Peace reigned again for about two minutes, then we heard singing from the beach, so we went down to investigate. Silhouetted in the moonlight was a group of people sitting in a circle, two with guitars, singing in beautiful four-part harmony. It took me a minute to realise that they were all men. Uh, oh. But no, they were adamant that I should stay. They said it was fine because I am not from their village.

It transpired that they were farewelling two of their number who were leaving the next morning on the plane. Tuba was freely shared, and they offered it to me. I drank with the men, and sang along as well.

Much of the music was sacred, but some was really bawdy and fun. It was one of those moments you know you will remember for a lifetime, or what's left of it anyway. It was magic, and then it got better. Our friend Glen picked up a guitar and played! I couldn't believe it. His fingers, so crushed only a few weeks earlier, were now playing a guitar, and beautifully. I got a bit teary at that one.

Soon all the men were summoned by their women for food, prayers and farewell speeches, and we were invited along. The festivities took place among the graves. On Mogmog graves are dotted around the houses and are adorned with masses of silk floral tributes. People want their beloved family with them after death. Andrew and I didn't stay long; we didn't think it was our place. But it was a lovely evening.

I went off to bed, and Andrew, as he frequently does, went in search of a drinking buddy. He found Glen then came back to get me out of bed to join them — another thing he frequently does! No kebabs, though. Miss them! They go so well with drunken ramblings.

This particular drunken ramble was very enlightening. I now had a clearer understanding of the Mike incident. During World War II, the last male chief of Mogmog died, leaving four daughters and no sons. This would not do! According to tradition, the chief must be a man who is ratified by the village matriarch. Consequently, the island was chiefless while the people worked out what to do; there was no quick solution to the problem. Meanwhile one of the daughters also died. Of the remaining family, the eldest daughter had daughters only, as did the next daughter. Finally, the last daughter produced a son as her youngest child.

By then, as so much time had elapsed, Juanito had been made chief as he was the eldest hunting male on Mogmog and, coincidentally, has the role of turtle divider for the village. Now, however, there are four distinct clans who, for varying reasons, believe they have claim to the chiefdom. This divides things in the village, particularly late at night after much tuba has been consumed. Mike, Raymond and Glen are all from the one clan, and their grandfather is the only son from the four daughters of the last male chief. This guy lives happily in Hawaii and wants nothing to do with chiefdom, which isn't helping. His family, however, feels that his existence proves their supremacy. You can see why this only comes out after dark.

Mike is a volatile guy, to say the least, and he insulted a member of another clan one too many times over a few too many tubas. Raymond clonking him with a torch sent the signal that his clan had dealt with Mike, and thereby removed the ability of any other clan to administer discipline. It has been done; it can't be redone. The feeling here is that Mike may well have been killed if Raymond had not got in there first. And the punishment needed to be seen to be sufficient, hence the hardness of the clonk!

Now why didn't I think of all that?

After the night of Mike's punishment, once everyone cooled down, the men got together and decided as a village that Mike cannot drink for six months and must do community service of some kind for the duration. If he is a good Vegemite, they will review it in three months. Mike is quietly agreeing to his sentence.

SIXTEEN

KIDS MATTER

Woke this morning to find Shanni's bike out the front of the house, wrecked. The pedals had been snapped off, and the chain was wrapped and jammed. Totally unusable. We bought it for her for her eighth birthday. It has travelled to four countries and crossed thousands of sea miles. But in no time at all on Mogmog, it's a wreck.

A few days ago, Andrew oiled and serviced it, and with misgivings we let the kids ride it. This was against Andrew's better judgement in particular.

Yesterday, at 6.30 in the morning, Diana was woken by one of the kids calling through her bedroom window, wanting to use the bike; this morning there was dead silence. The local kids *knew* the bike had been wrecked, yet no one said a word. No one came up to apologise, or ask if they could do anything to help fix it. I am furious about that.

This comes hot on the heels of an unpleasant incident last week, when someone took a knife to our inflatable turtle and severed the flipper. This turtle had been used by all the kids for weeks, but someone took a knife and ended all the fun. We said that as a consequence, no one would get to use the Rip Stiks, which are a kind of skateboard, until someone owned up to destroying the turtle. The kids were very quick to point the finger, but we thought the 'no one gets it till someone owns up' strategy might be the fairest.

One of the men pulled me aside and said that it wouldn't work. When I asked why not, his response was that the kid who did it is happy to have done it, and is happy to be denying the other kids use of the turtle, so therefore would never own up. So far, a week later, he is right.

Okay, I can hear you thinking, it's only a stupid bike and a stupid turtle, and, hey, you're right. I can also hear you saying, 'But you have everything and they have nothing'; you're right again. *But!*

I remember an Aboriginal elder from Arnhem Land once holding up two $20 notes in his hands, and he said words to the effect of, 'Do you see these two notes? Do you know the difference between these two notes? This one was given to me but this one — this one — this one I earned. Do you know which one is the most important to me? … This is the problem with the Aboriginal situation today.'

And you know what? He's right. If you earn it, it's important. If you don't, it's not. And these people seem to have no respect for anything — not *anything* — because everything they have has been given to them.

Perhaps we have been doing too much giving ourselves? In the last few weeks we've bought four ukeleles and given them to Juanito for kids in the village who might like them but can't afford them; we have organised a fun 'bring out your pig' day, where we are providing prizes; we have paid for a boat to go out for the day, and Andrew and Juanito caught enough fish to feed the whole island; we have made a cake and shared it around.

* * *

Largely, there is little in the way of active parenting on Mogmog. Kids run around all day and appear to attend school only when they wish. There have been numerous times that I have asked kids why they are not at school and have got a plethora of plausible lies in return. They have open innocent faces, and they look you straight in the eye and say whatever pops into their heads.

Their parents are never seen, not even to make sure the kids are safe or fed or whatever, let alone to teach them basic manners. There are kids who walk into the house — never knock — sit down and tell me what to do.

Jarrod is one of these bossy ones. A couple of times he's waltzed in, sat down, and yelled at the other kids visiting the house to get out. He is the rudest child I have ever met, but he is not alone.

'Has your mother taught you manners?' I ask him.

'No,' comes the response; the expression adds 'As if! What's with *you*?'

'You'll have to learn manners if you come to this house,' I say.

He laughs in my face. I tell him to get out. He refuses. At the end of my tether, I yell at him to get out *now*, which startles him out of the place.

That was several visits ago. We are now making slow progress.

I have had kids yell at me in our house because I pronounced a word wrong. I have had kids demand a hot chocolate, or just help themselves to what they want. Our things are constantly 'going west'. During the last week alone, the eight kitchen knives we were supplied with have disappeared from the washing up; Diana's paints have been stolen — someone must have come through her bedroom window — and a man's thu was thrown onto Diana's bed (don't know what that was about). Stuff outside is obviously fair game: the stack of wood Andrew is using for boat repairs is being used by kids as toys, and every day the stack is scattered all over the undercover area, with all the smaller bits stolen by the kids.

One of the kids here is a boy named Persley who suffers badly from epilepsy. His frequent seizures have caused him great mental trauma, and he has difficulty talking and making himself understood. The kids treat him abominably. They yell, they push, they tell him to get out, they laugh at him and, as a result, the kid has no self-confidence — which worsens his ability to gain confidence, learn language and be part of his community. Persley is a thoroughly nice and good person.

We have taken him under our wings a bit, and he follows me and the girls around or spends hours with Andrew, watching him work on the boat. He has been growing in confidence, and will now ask questions, find out the English word for different things. It's great to see him blossoming. He has a perpetual grin.

Persley spends all day, other than school time, with us, which is absolutely fine, but where are his parents? They never check to make sure he's okay. They never ask us if we're okay with him being around so much; they probably don't know he's here. This kid, of all the kids, needs parental care. Where the hell is it?

Kids seem almost like trophies. Young men — teenagers often — walk around with their kids as a badge of honour, but there it ends. I have had mothers coming up to me saying they would like to visit, but they can't control their kids, so they don't come.

Some adults make a sincere effort with the kids, and a lot of the older women who are now grandmothers do genuinely try and care for them. What will happen when their moderating, caring and largely ineffective voice is no longer there?

In Australia it is the norm that parents know where kids are, care where kids are, and teach them values, discipline and manners, and as a result kids know the consequences of their actions. In short, it is a society that cares. Not this one. I dread what will happen when these kids grow up and become the adults of this society.

Tell you what … don't get shipwrecked here in 20 years' time!

* * *

Juanito is well aware of the issues. We don't tell him everything that goes on, but he knows. He genuinely despairs. But even his own son has left his child to live with Juanito and his wife, Ellie, on a full-time basis to be educated. He visits every secondish weekend. Juanito says sometimes he wakes up to find his glasses gone or the radio volume knob pulled off. He is a kind, kind man, but he is not making inroads because parents take no responsibility for their kids.

Raymond is in a similar situation to Juanito; he has care of his nephew, Rio, while his sister is in the Philippines. He is tearing his hair out. As we know, Raymond is a 'do it' guy — just ask Mike — but he is making no inroads with the boy. Rio hangs with Jarrod, and the two of them attend school once a week on average. More than once I have seen Raymond yelling at Rio and telling him to go to school, so Rio goes off in the direction of school and comes home at the end of the day. But he hasn't been to school; his teacher told us. Raymond has full-time work, so there is a limit to what he can physically do to keep an eye on Rio.

* * *

At any one time, there are usually four to six kids at our place. I have no space. They like to jump on our mattress and paint with acrylic paints, and are also likely to pick up anything they can and slip out the door with it, especially Diana's iPod. Even though these visitors are pretty disruptive, it goes right against my nature to tip them out. It sits wrong with me not to trust and not to welcome kids openly into the house. At home in Perth we would have the same number of kids over and it would be a happy, raucous, polite, laughing affair, with kids that I have grown to love sincerely, so it really goes against the grain for me to act the big green meany.

Andrew is more pragmatic than me. He has seen the writing on the wall for ages, and has been dead against all the open-door stuff and the sharing of toys and anything else. Now that the bike has been wrecked, while he hasn't come out with 'I told you so', I sense in him a very real anger that will take days to simmer down.

I know this boy. When he's unhappy, head for the hills.

* * *

Andrew has now prepared the hulls so that a structure can be erected within the gaping hole that extends all down the starboard hull. He has placed a single beam of timber at the base of where the hull should be along the length of the hull. He uses this as a point from which to work.

Next Andrew will attack the bulkheads. After the shipwreck, parts of some remained and can be reconstructed, while others had completely gone and will need to be started from scratch. Once the bulkheads are fixed, strips of timber can be attached to them, and the hull will begin to slowly take shape.

Mike often comes down to watch. He sits silently, watches what is being done, and then, when he can, he starts doing the same as Andrew or maybe handing Andrew whatever tool he will need next. Then, without a word, he will wander off and we won't see him for a day or so.

SEVENTEEN

A FLAT PATCH

Right now it's 10pm Friday. Andrew's not here, and the kids are in bed — not asleep but in bed. I'm drinking red wine. I have always believed, and it has been proven true so many times — though not everyone agrees — that what you really feel is brought out by a few drinks. So here are my Friday night ramblings.

This evening after dinner, Andrew and I went to visit Glen of the hand fame. He wasn't home, but Kena, his lovely lady, was. She had babysitters organised as she was about to head off to meet Glen, and invited us to come along. Off we went, to find Glen in a group of men where women were not welcome. I quickly backed off, as did Kena, and I told Andrew that he should stay.

Kena is a lovely, articulate, funny lady who teaches everything at the school. She and Glen have two kids, one of whom has behavioural issues. She won't marry Glen, and he can't go to

Pohnpei, where Kena comes from, as he has child abuse charges against him. They stem from his prior relationship with a 15-year-old when he was 20.

The two of us chatted as we retraced our footsteps, then we said goodnight to each other. And here I am: the men of Mogmog party and the women just sit at home.

Earlier tonight, I was sitting on the front step and witnessed Jarrod, who everyone knows is a nasty kid, and Sith from next door throwing puppies to each other. I was horrified. Every time they missed, the pups would fall to the ground from 6 feet. My tears are streaming just writing about it.

Straight away, I ran over and balled them out. They looked at me mystified. 'But we only eat them anyway; what's the problem?'

How can I accept that? Ranting like a lunatic, I took the puppies off the boys and delivered them back to their mum. Sith's involvement shocked me, as his family have Rolande, a beautiful honey-and-white pooch with a very soft face and nature.

Rolande and I became mates when I rescued her week-old pups; they'd got caught behind some wood and couldn't get back to her. She yelped and yipped, and I helped. Then we had a magic moment: I left her to it, and she raced after me and jumped up on me, crashing into my hip, and then charged back to her pups. It was a real thanks!

Of course there's a big repercussion coming for me now. The father of Sith, the kid I ballsed out, had just today offered us well water from his tap. It was no idle offer; it mean no more well washing, water on the garden, but then I yell at his kid.

Next thing, Andrew arrives from the boat, sees me upset and asks what happened. When I tell him, he stomps over to Sith, picks him up by a foot, asks him how he likes it, and says he's going to get a mate so they can play 'chuck the kid'. I'm pleased Andrew stood up for me and our values, but at the same time we're a lone and wrong voice in their culture. Upsetting.

* * *

I can trace back further through my day and find so many more things to get wound up about. Today I got on the phone and tried to organise the delivery of fibreglass sorted, and despite my best efforts I couldn't make it happen. It's not that I can't get hold of the items; it's just that I couldn't sort out freight costs and despatch. The guy Paul found in Guam has proved to be useless: great at promises and words but very ineffective, so we have had to give up on him.

Waiting on mail is agony right now. My sister, Lindy, posted a pack five weeks ago; no pack yet. After Tuesday there's no schoolwork for the girls to go on with. I can rig something up, but that will put them behind. They are going so well; I don't want the ball to stop rolling. There is a school production tomorrow night so the kids are rehearsing and performing. As a result, there won't be a boat from Falalop this weekend. That's way too disproportionately disheartening.

To top things off, Andrew and I are almost out of alcohol. PMA won't fly it in because that would go against everything they are trying to achieve. Is it just me or are religious groups totally out of step when it comes to practicality? The ship brings alcohol for those who can afford it. The locals can't afford bottled bevvies but then again they're happy with tuba, which they make on a daily basis, then get smashed and smash each other. So the PMA ban flying in alcohol for the other … oh, yeah, just the two of us! What's with that? How fucking impractical is that! Idealism at its religious best!

Seeing as how I'm a roll with complaints, I'll add that the freezer on the ship is shagged and has been for weeks. But let's not fix it! Oh, no! It's way easier to say it's stuffed and be done with it.

As for getting meat in the next order, I'm trying for Eskies and ice. I'll keep you posted.

It's Jolene's birthday today, so I thought we'd do the nice thing. This morning the girls and I made chocolate brownies with our last brownie mix and iced it with the last of our icing, and took it down to her and Raymond's place, singing 'Happy Birthday'.

'Thanks' was the response. Not 'Hi, how are you?' Not 'That's so nice of you!' Just a half-hearted 'Thanks' as Jolene continued to weave. She didn't even stop or turn around. The girls found that very disheartening.

Wait, there's more. Stanley wanted guitar strings so I rang a shop in Perth called Theo's Music. It's a business I have dealt with since I was 11. I have known Miles the owner since he used to help his dad out during school holidays. I taught flute in their studios for eight years. A guy named Daniel took my order; all fine.

Then a message came through: I need to speak to Steve in

accounts. He wants an EFT transfer. Now I can get Sue to do that, but what's wrong with my Visa? It's been fine for them every other time. But no, because of the risk of fraud, they will not take a phone Visa order for more than $50. Miles is on leave, so I can't talk to him directly. The staff SMSed him, and no, they will not send me the guitar strings.

They want Lindy to go in there and pay in person, but *then* they require proof of delivery. *Hello!* I tried in vain to explain where I was, and that there is no such thing as proof of delivery. So much for building a business relationship. Even after 30 years or more of customer loyalty, that's what happens. Hmmm! I'll give Graham at Concept a call on Monday.

* * *

Here I am, still sitting with my red wine on this Friday night. Now I'm mulling over some new thoughts. Andrew came back with Glen and a couple of others. Glen was pretty smashed, and began telling me again about his convictions. He also told me he spent five years in Year 9 but never finished school, even though he wanted to make more of himself, and that he is passionate about artwork. Nature and tattooing are his great loves. In gaol he made a living drawing tattoos.

While I was listening to him very carefully, it hit me: this man has ADHD! Dear idiot — that took you a while! I'm no shrink, but I know ADHD well because for many years I have watched a dear friend deal with it. I have seen my friend get in and out of scrapes, battle with authority, struggle with study and fixate most fixedly on whatever the project at hand happens to be — just like Glen fixates on the boat! He and Glen could be brothers.

I have also witnessed the positive difference it can make to an adult man to be diagnosed and receive proper treatment. There is so much angst and frustration inherent in the condition that need not be a part of life; the constant temptation to flout authority and tussle with authority need not be there. And, most importantly, in my experience, there is under the mantle of ADHD a thoroughly good person with a true heart who craves to be understood. Glen is totally in love with his lady, yet she won't marry him. Yet Kena loves him; she told me so.

Their son is at times unmanageable as well. Could he also have ADHD? It's a strong possibility. It's not, I believe, inherited as such, but there is certainly a propensity for the condition within families. I wonder if there is some way we can help him.

I asked Glen when he was here, 'Do you get things stuck in your head, and do you worry them and worry them and not let them go?'

He looked at me as if he'd been stung.

'When you are working on something, does it get in your head, so you can't think of anything else? Do you wake up at night thinking about it, and nothing else?'

He stared deep into my eyes, with tears in his, and said, 'How do you know this?'

My heart went out to him. I've got to give this one some thought. Maybe there's a way.

EIGHTEEN

MOTHER'S DAY

Mother's Day is a big thing on Mogmog. Presents are not exchanged but sentiments most definitely are. Even though Andrew and I had planned for the four of us to take the dinghy and go to a neighbouring island for the day — to swim, snorkel and catch a picnic lunch of fish or coconut crab — Juanito had other ideas.

The day before Mother's Day, we went to his house for a drink. We were there for about an hour, and he had clearly had his share of tuba when he announced to us that Andrew and he would cook Mother's Day lunch for Ellie and me and the kids. He wanted Andrew to come back to his place in the morning and they'd shoot two chickens. Sigh; okay. The kids were a bit mutinous, but hey, they've been mutinous before; they'll get over it.

While we were there, Juanito also stated that he had decided on names for the girls. Some time ago, he said that he wanted to give the girls a Mogmog name each that he felt was appropriate to them. It signifies that they will always be a part of Mogmog. After some weeks' deliberation, he had now come to some conclusions and we were to approve this before he went ahead with the next step.

As yet I don't know the Mogmog names, and Juanito will write them out for me, but he has decided that Shan is to be 'younger daughter of the wind', and Diana is to be 'older daughter of the ocean between islands'. We were a bit overwhelmed by this, and we obviously love the names and approved them on the spot, although he wanted us to think about them first.

Also that night, all within that one-hour get-together, we decided that the girls' school in Perth, Kyilla Primary School, could become a sister school for Mogmog Elementary School, swapping cultures and ideas, and sending resources and values in both directions. I know a number of Kyilla young ladies who would benefit greatly from understanding that no, the world won't end if you don't have the pink ones!

All in all, it was a good night.

Next morning, I was bombarded in bed by two flying daughters who told me to stay put and wait. In came a box of lovingly created artwork: beautiful cards, a hand-painted rose in a homemade frame, a shell collage, a silver leaf for good luck, a shell mouse, a shell hedgehog, and a beautiful paint-by-numbers creation of Chook's, full of ducks, irises, trees and a lake with beautiful reflections and huge attention to detail. I spent ages arranging it all around the room and putting up the things that needed to be on the wall. Now, wherever I look, there is a homemade reminder of my girls and my Mogmog Mother's Day. Things like that really put the world in perspective, don't they?

After that, Andrew and I went to the beach with the air-rifle, where I'm sure I became the first topless Mogmog mother shooting at a cardboard box with a crayon cross target on it on Mother's Day. Got it, too! So did the great chook hunter, so he was pleased. At least now he felt confident he could put the poultry on the table for the Mother's Day meal Juanito had in mind for us all.

A busy program of events had been planned. Next we sat around waiting for Mass, which we had been told would be at 10am. Father Nick arrived from Falalop at about 9.30, but then nothing happened. Turned out that the men were busy butchering the 11 turtles that they had caught for Mother's Day the previous day, so Father Nick had taken advantage of the situation, and was down at the school principal's place getting drunk! The world was a happy place. We could have done our picnic and no one would have been the wiser! It was 2pm before Father Nick made his way to the altar. No one cared. Hey, it's Mother's Day! Everywhere I went, everyone knew I'm a mother, so everyone greeted me with a big cheery, 'Happy Mother's Day, Jen!' It was really lovely.

Anyway, come 2 o'clock, back to church we all went. The girls had also made me frangipani leis and a head wreath, so I was beautifully decked out. I plonked myself down again on the concrete floor, next to Rocky the dog, topless as usual, and found myself looking at the most wonderful array of flowers ever. The flowers in church are always an amazing work of art, but that day it was a riot of frangipani, bougainvillea and other tropical flowers, and a blaze of vibrant colour.

At the end of Mass, while everyone was still seated, several men stood up and gave every mother a frangi lei, which was a lovely touch, and then Juanito got to his feet. Holding two specially made leis and floral headpieces, the really intricate and heavy ones, he walked over to Ellie, his lovely wife, and placed one of each on her.

Those two are very special together. The love between them is a palpable thing: you can practically see and feel it in the air around them. Things like that always turn me to goo. So I was sitting there all goo at those two when Juanito walked over to me and gently placed the other lei around my neck and the floral wreath on my head.

It was totally unexpected. I was pretty overcome, not only by the gesture, but by the look on his face and the smile in his eyes as he did it. I looked at Andrew sitting next to me, and he was blinking back tears. It was one of those moments I'll never forget.

Back out in the sunshine, Andrew went off to perform his chicken duty. Never done that one before. He came back all smug, but a quick scratch of the surface showed he was pleased not to have made an idiot of himself, and glad he got them both first time.

Dinner a few hours later consisted of turtle rissoles, chicken curry with rice and fresh bread. Don't tell anyone from Greenpeace, but it was great!

During the course of the evening, Juanito and Andrew plotted the now imminent Inaugural Ulithian Ham Smoker, which will be bigger than Ben Hur. Our dear friend Glenys has given us the secret recipe and the secret method, and Andrew is building the smoker. Juanito is beside himself with excitement. It's a big secret, and Juanito's determined to perfect his ham-making then unveil it to the Ulithian world. He can't get the grin off his face. Hope it works!

The day of the great ham smoke-off is also the daughter naming day, so it should be a biggie. When we left that night, Juanito was blinking back tears — I guess it was his turn — saying that he didn't know what he is going to do without us.

So ended a Mother's Day I can never forget!

* * *

Next morning was all systems go. Into it and onto it! Andrew's job: get on with the boat. Jenny's jobs: finalise all fibreglass and resin needs with a company named ATL Composites in Brisbane. Appoint and coordinate freight-forwarding of the same, with the aim to get the goods on Wednesday's Pacific Flier flight to Palau. (We'd met Reg and Helen at a party in Palau when they were first setting up Pacific Flier, offering affordable flights between Brisbane and Palau. Helen subsequently became friends with

Val, my stepmother, and when she heard our Mogmog story, she immediately rang Val to offer cheap freight to help us out.) Organise guitar strings for Stanley for the choir or for him to on-sell apparently (Ellie calls him a sweet-lipped emperor!). But wait, there's more: I need to get the Yap post office to forward our mail to Mogmog; finalise our account with the Yap shop; finalise our order with the Yap shop; and organise for the frozen meat to be freighted in newly purchased Eskies, and to be packed with ice, as the ship that is leaving Yap for us next Monday night has a stuffed freezer.

Guess what? It's a public holiday in Yap, so forget most of the list.

Success with the meat! Yay. Don't quite know how we would have coped without our beef and chicken supplies. Yes, we eat turtle, but it's not the diet of choice, and we've never been huge fish eaters. Mind you, if it came to it, we'd have to be, wouldn't we!

Got a hold of a guy named Anthony at ATL Composites, and he put together the list of everything we needed. Great! He costed it all, and we were very happy with what he came up with. When we talked with the people at Pacific Flier, we found out that their preferred freight-forwarder was CT Logistics. Rang them and spoke with a guy called Les. Turns out ATL are also clients of CT, and that Les deals with Anthony all the time. No need for explanations or phone numbers or anything!

Paul, our friend and number-one technical support person in Perth, had emailed over the weekend, so we had Pacific Flier's freight rates. It was then that we realised what a wonderful deal we were being given by Reg and Helen. They want $3 per kilo, as opposed to the going rate of $415 a kilo. (Even though the rate drops significantly if you have any larger quantities, it never gets anywhere near $3!)

Based on this rate, we decided to send the whole lot by air to Palau, rather than wait for a ship, and I'm betting that we wouldn't get as low as $3 per kilo on a ship anyway.

So this morning our fibreglass and resin was picked up from the warehouse in the Gold Coast and taken to Brizzie to hopefully get on tomorrow night's flight. Bet it won't work like that, but even if it doesn't, it's only a week until we'll have it!

Freight and fibreglass sorted. Meat on boat sorted.

In and around all of the above organising — bear in mind the sat phone fall-outs and the time wasted in HF transmissions — I'd also lined up a day's schoolwork for the girls. That side of things was getting trickier by the day, so I also emailed Deb, the girls' teacher, and told her we are out of work as the mail hasn't come.

By the time I surfaced to see what Andrew was up to, he was sitting on the ground with Raymond looking particularly smug. Something was cooking! The two of them had spent the morning repairing the alternator for the town generator. It turned out to be pretty complicated so took longer than Andrew had expected, but that wasn't all they'd managed to do. There was Andrew, grinning like a Cheshire cat at the hull in front of him! He had finished the inside of the starboard hull structure. By that I mean that the timber was all glued in place waiting for glass roving and epoxy resin coating. The hull on the inside was back.

Andrew and I sat beaming at each other; we were getting there. To celebrate, we each cracked a beer. I hate beer, but, hey, there was no wine, and the tuba Stanley had provided — all 1 litre of it, in exchange for the guitar strings — was warm. So beer it had to be. It's not really that bad, is it?

We sat and started contemplating where we should go next. What a wonderful feeling. No more 'if', just 'when'. And not too far off, either.

Maybe very soon, depending on the mail. And the airfreight. And the cost. And — who cares; it'll happen.

NINETEEN

AT THE TWO-MONTH MARK

Time is flying by. It's now late May, two months since we landed on this island. And I can't believe it's only a week since I last wrote! So much has happened.

As planned, the glass and resin made it all the way from Brisbane to Palau on Wednesday night. How 'bout that! Les, the freight-forwarder from Brisbane for CTI Logistics, is fantastic.

I spoke to our Palau-based friends Dennis and Sam, with a view to getting the shipment on the next day's flight to Yap. It was all looking good. I rang Pacific Missionary Aviation (PMA) and told them to expect it. They were set to catch the freight and get it to the ship that's supposed to arrive here by sea on 18th June. I rang Dennis, the skipper, and he said he would accept the goods at any time right up until they left at 4pm and that they would charge $20 all up. Fantastic! A plan. I love plans!

Then I heard again from Sam in Palau and suddenly it was 'Ummm, no!' The goods were stuck in customs, as Continental Airlines needed safety documentation on the non-hazardous epoxy to prove that it was non-hazardous. How very Palau! So, that was the end of that plan.

Eventually, the goods cleared customs, and our glass and resin are now in Yap, in Amos's possession. Genuine progress!

Andrew went to Falalop this morning to meet Amos, and he will rummage through the shipment to get the glue and one pack of resin and bring them when he returns on Monday. The next ship to Yap arrives on 4th June, which is Saturday week, and then we will have the remainder.

We can work with that.

Now that we know we're onto a good thing with the team of Les and Pacific Flier, we've been busy. We asked Yanmar to reroute the engine parts to Brizzie for the following week's flight. This they happily did. Then we found a stainless steel company in Perth who had the rudder shaft steel we needed. They cut it and sent it to Brizzie, and that too made the Wednesday flight. Then Valli, my wicked stepmother, said she was sending us a pack, and that also made it to the flight. It weighs 50 kilos apparently! What the hell has she sent!

Another call we made was to our great mate 'Bones' in Brizzie. He is a Qantas captain, so has a lot of holidays; he's on a five-week break right now, and happily agreed to go to Bunnings and get bits and pieces for us. Talk about the cherry on the cupcake: he also got that to Les for Wednesday. You gotta love your mates!

But wait, there's more. The final part of our glass order was cut and ready on Tuesday, so it made it to the flight too. Les was waiting to catch the lot, and he did!

All that is now in Palau, and Dennis is probably sitting bemusedly in the middle of it all. His plan is to post it all on to us in one hit, keeping the rudder shafts for himself. Thanks, Dennis!

Adding to the mix of stuff happening in the last week, problems with the post came to a head. The mail had been slow in coming through, to the point that it was getting ridiculous. We had still not received mail from six weeks ago. Last Friday, we received one box: Diana's schoolwork. None for Shan. Of course Shan thought that was great, but that was beside the point. I needed work for both girls; if one lot could come through, why hadn't the other? It made no sense!

The system is that the mail is flown into Falalop by Amos each Friday. The post office is in the terminal building, in a small room with a metal roller door. The PO is open only when the plane is there. Each Friday, the guys from Mogmog go to Falalop to meet the plane and get the mail. Then they go to the high school when classes finish and pick up the Mogmog kids and bring them home for the weekend.

I asked Glen if he would go to the post office and check whether we had mail. He promised me he would look in person. At about the time the group arrived back from Falalop, I met him on the boat and asked him how he'd got on. 'Captain Plausible' looked me earnestly in the eye, said he went and asked and that there was nothing else for us. Sigh.

A few minutes later, I ran into Andrew, and his story was different. Glen had told him that he hadn't checked the mail because the post office had been locked! We both saw red.

I went back to *Windrider*, cranked up the satellite phone and rang the Yap post office. They assured me, for the third time, that two items at least had gone from them in each of the last three weeks.

Okay. Who's not coming clean here? I rang PMA and spoke to Esther, the person I usually dealt with, and she said that she had spoken to Amos, and he had personally taken two boxes to the Falalop PO. He even remembered that they were both school book boxes. Aha! That meant that the missing link was between the plane and Mogmog.

By this point, Andrew was furious. He stormed off to see Raymond and announced that he had had enough and that he was going to call the Yap police and report a federal offence. Raymond responded with, 'Okay, okay, okay, okay, I'll sort it out.' Andrew stomp, stomp, stomped off, and we waited to see what would happen.

Two hours later, Raymond arrived in the doorway with a wheelbarrow chokkers with mail. The rotters had been blatantly lying for weeks as our mail stockpiled all the while at Falalop. Week after week, I had asked the guys and they had looked straight at me with those earnest brown eyes and told me that no, there was nothing this week. Bastards! And get this! Glen had gone to the PO with the wheelbarrow and filled it up, and he was so excited to deliver all this stuff to us. Hadn't he done us a wonderful favour? Go figure. I just don't get it. What is the

Windrider looking great in our beloved Palau before leaving for Yap and Mogmog.

Dolphins are regular friends while on passage.

One of these guys came over and gently rose vertically to touch Diana's hand. Wow!

This was the afternoon before the typhoon.

Locals clearing out the boat on the morning of the shipwreck. Mike, in the foreground, is already wearing Andrew's board shorts.

Pulling *Windie* out of the water and onto the beach; it was the islanders versus the boat.

Andrew was instantly
— and always —
accepted by the men
of Mogmog.

Thankfully, Diana and Shannon appeared to come through the
ordeal unscathed.

'The Graduate', who
was dinner at the high
school graduation.

Finally, she is off the ground and at a workable height.

The holey hull.

Our low-tech jacking system.
But, hey, it was all we had.

Juanito, looking
laid back.

The workbench.

Work in progress
— the windlass.

Everything was
full of coral.

Mike — there
to the end.

Our temporary
home on
Mogmog

Kids being kids.

Another beautiful Mogmog sunset.

Shannon watching the supply ship; these became our lifeline when they actually arrived.

Some locals pulling live turtles up the beach.

Before Andrew started work on the galley, you could see right through to the ground beneath.

No more al fresco kitchen.

It was a great day when we could use the galley again.

Over several months we went from having a ruined hull ...

... to having a restored hull

Mogmog's shop.

We were all expected at church each week.

Preparing
for a feast.

While Chofung lay dead, kids frolicked in the water nearby.

Our daughters — with Chofa, Chofung's long-time love — keeping vigil next to the cross they erected for poor Chofung.

Father Moses, a Mogmog-born priest, received a huge welcome the day he said his first Mass on the island.

The men performing a frenetic stick dance.

Mogmog women dancing for Father Moses's inaugural Mass.

The primary school graduation was another big day.

Andrew demonstrating
the results of the
shipwreck diet.

Notice the detail in
Shannon's beautiful
floral head dress.

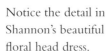

Traditional
Mother's Day
finery.

Moggie Doggie stole our
hearts and is now part of
the Barrie household.

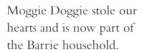

Carrying the engine on a pole.

The drums have been affixed to the hull to provide flotation — hopefully to get *Windie* over the reef at high tide.

While Andrew was awaiting parts for *Windrider*, he repaired this traditional boat and presented it to Juanito just before we left.

Helping winch the engine to Andrew, who is up on deck.

Moggie, an integral part of our tribe.

angle here? Are they waiting till we leave to use our mail (as it has become increasingly apparent they are doing with everything else they have stolen so far), or is it a mind game thing, some sort of power play, designed to wear us down and thence give up, leaving them with the boat at the end of the game?

Leaving that aside, suddenly it was Christmas! In the boxes we received — joy, oh joy! — a pair each of polaroid sunnies; Andrew's prescription glasses; books; five family blocks of Cadbury chocolate; canned vegies and fruits; a care pack from Loulou for the girls filled with zany glasses, muesli bars, girlie mags, funky rings, funky bracelets and funky all sorts of other stuff; Shan's schoolwork; over 100 DVDs of movies and our favourite TV series to watch on the computer; and everything was packed with lollies as padding. Everyone dived in and started unwrapping. It was raining lollies! It was a fantastic day! We argued over which chocolate to open, which movie to watch, and which food to eat. It was fantastic! Where would we be without our wonderful friends and family!

* * *

Andrew has been plugging away at the boat, and as of today, the wood structure for the hulls is complete. There are no more gaps, Charlie. It still needs the glass and resin, and a whole heap more finishing, but the hull is whole again: we have a whole, holeless, whole hull!

Gotta love that too. This means that Andrew has run out of boat stuff to do for the time being. So, it's on to Juanito's smoker.

TWENTY

LINES IN THE SAND

Yesterday we farewelled a friend.

Chofung was a beautiful, young, gentle-natured dog. She had six pups and a longtime live-in lover. She also had the great misfortune of living with Jarrod's family. I've talked already about Jarrod, the rude boy.

When we first met Chofung, she was incredibly timid. Her demeanour was defensive in the extreme. She was a small, brown, very fluffy girl, about 2 feet long and 18 inches high at the hip. Her boyfriend was Chofa; they were inseparable. You would always see them happily trotting behind their owner, Falalai, a great big, tall, proud-looking man, who has the fathering skills of a gnat!

Yesterday was Sunday. It was a perfectly calm day, the sky a deep vivid blue, no clouds, and the ocean was glassy in varying shades of turquoise. After church, the girls wanted a swim, so off they went happily, boogie boards flying. I followed a little later. When I got to our favourite swimming spot, Shan was crying and unintelligibly trying to tell me something. I heard the word Chofung in there with all the other sounds. Oh, no! They pointed down the beach. I told them not to follow me, and went to investigate.

I will never forget the sight awaiting me. Kids were playing in the water, about 20 metres from where Chofung lay lifelessly. There were drag marks through the sand which led to her final spot. A rope was tightly tied around her neck, which must have been used for dragging her along. Her right eye, which was staring ahead of her, showed signs of internal bleeding and slightly bulged from its socket. Her head was sunken in at the top. In the centre of the depression was a bloody and deep bludgeon mark.

A short time later, it was here, standing in front of beautiful Chofung, that Andrew found me crying in anger. I don't know which emotion was stronger: an all-encompassing anger or deep sadness at the cruelty and the unnecessary death of a wonderful creature.

Together, we went back to the girls and confirmed their fears. Diana told us she'd seen what she'd taken to be a pig being dragged down to the beach, but then realised it was Chofung. We made the girls promise not to go down to where she lay. The reality was much worse than the imagined in this case.

It wasn't yet lunchtime at this stage, and we all headed off. Later I discovered that that dog stayed there in the hot sun, while children laughed and played over and around her, for hours and hours. No one came to collect her until about 4pm.

For weeks Jarrod had been goading all of us, saying how they were going to kill her and butcher her. About six rumoured execution days had come and gone, but last night that little dog became dinner. She would have had 3 or 4 pounds of meat on her — if that.

* * *

Andrew and I needed to take stock of what had just taken place, so we headed for our favourite spot — a sewer, as it happens, situated between our new and very experimental vegie garden, and our salubrious accommodation — with a scotch and Tang, to calm down and talk through what — if anything — we could do. By coincidence, the day before we had been on the front page of the *Sydney Morning Herald* — must've been a slow news day. We hadn't anticipated this publicity, but hey, it gave us an idea. Maybe we could use the media to promote awareness in Australia of this hideous practice, and thereby bring pressure to bear here in Mogmog.

We made a few other decisions while we were at it. This incident has made us more determined than ever to get *Windie* repaired ASAP so we can leave. Time to ramp this thing up, but no more involving the locals. By now we had come to the realisation that we wanted no sense of obligation to these people, and that we could no longer accept their ethics and principles as our own. In short the respect, and thus the level of friendship, had sadly deteriorated.

From now on, there'll be no more handouts to the locals. Earlier in the week, we had literally given them the shirts that weren't on our backs. But there'll be no more gestures like that, and no more purchasing for the locals in the Yap stores. It's time for us to close ranks and fend for ourselves, and if that means moving back onto the boat, so be it.

It was a plan, and we got straight onto it. I emailed Amos and asked if we could start getting our stuff delivered at his convenience, rather than waiting for the ship. His response was immediate. He has decided to deliver everything right away; all our glass, resin and other stuff that has come via Brisbane. That means today, as I write.

The girls wrote letters to the editor, which we emailed to both the *Sydney Morning Herald* and to the *West Australian*. Unfortunately, ABC Radio's 'Macca' had finished for the day, but we'll contact him next week.

Then we turned our attention to the locals and trying to change things here. Andrew made a simple pine cross. The girls and I gathered flowers, and we went to where Chofung's remains had been dumped. We placed the cross and arranged the flowers. People asked us who it was for. We told them, and then, to our surprise, a lady came up with a single flower and asked if she could put it there too. There were tears.

Without a word, suddenly Andrew leapt up and disappeared. Over the next hour or so, people of all ages came up quietly and placed simple flowers or beautiful arrangements on Chofung's resting place. I was overwhelmed. More tears flowed.

When Falalai came back from fishing, Andrew was still roaming the streets floralising the place, and so I perhaps stupidly yelled at Falalai to enjoy his dinner. A screaming match ensued.

'I didn't kill my dog!'

'No, you're so gutless you had to have someone else do it for you!'

'I have to feed my family.'

'Catch a *fucking fish*!'

And so it went on. The men who heard this exchange thought it was hilarious. I was maintaining control, but just. Falalai left.

By the time Andrew came back, the mound of flowers around the cross was about 1 foot high and 2 feet across. People came to just sit. Someone made a shell heart with Chofung's name in it. Others wrote messages on the cross. Maybe we were getting the message through.

As the sun went down and the tide came up towards the flowers, three young boys asked to sit next to me. Clyde, who is 12, had something he wanted to tell me. Last year he went to Yap to stay with relations; it was his first trip away from his family, and he was very excited. Before he left, he said goodbye to his beloved 13-year-old dog, who had been his best friend for his whole life. Clyde wondered if he would see her again, and when he returned home a week later, he learned that his brother had killed the dog and that the family had eaten it. He didn't speak to them for over a month.

After Clyde had told me his awful story, he had the idea of praying for his dog. As he prayed aloud, tears ran down my face. Then one of his friends sang a hymn. So, as the flowers washed slowly out on the tide and the sun set on a peaceful ocean, we sat and joined the boys singing hymns for a lovely lady.

* * *

After dark, we had a run-in with Stanley when he told Andrew that I should have more respect for men. According to Stanley, as a man, Andrew needs to pull me into line. Women aren't allowed to drink here because, so we're told, they lose respect for their men when they drink. Say what they really feel, more like!

Stanley's timing was off; I wasn't going to cop this. I told him that no one in the village has respect for him, that he is referred to as a sweet-lipped emperor, and that I had been advised not to give him the guitar strings I had organised, as the general opinion was he would sell them to his friends, rather than giving them to the choir as he said he would. I told him respect was earned, and that he earned nothing.

Women should know their place, he replied, and if they didn't, men must discipline them. I couldn't believe my ears. I told him about the rest of the world, but forget it, that was going to do no good. Eventually Andrew told him to leave. Not pleasant.

There was more unpleasantness in store. A teenager screamed at me, 'It's our fucking island.' Then he physically attacked Andrew. His mates pulled him off.

Later that night, I rang the embassy, expressing concern about the incident with Chofung, and adding that not only were we unhappy with the situation here, but that we were concerned for our safety. Andrew rang our Perth-based friend Paul at home with the same message. Both said they would contact us in the morning.

Andrew slept on the boat that night; I stayed in the house. We each had a rifle with us in bed. That is the measure of the unrest that this issue has caused in the community.

Oi Platypuses,

I figured your comms went tits up! Nice to know you are all ok!

Surfing the net, I enjoy the reporter drama of y'all in the news having to go bush surviving off the occasional turtle (and related blood), fishies hand caught, finger-crushing crabs and runny poo coco juice! Hehehe, I thinks to myself ... they are out of BOOZE! (aww, the kids will be right mate, they still have flexible bones and low calorie requirements) ;-)

Have you sussed out how to monopolize the Mogmog tuba syndicate into Aussie control? A good stiff drink can be had from tapioca roots if you can find them ... helped the *Bounty* mutineers cope after the good stuff ran out. And rats are a delicacy in some particular back-woods of the world.

Well, if anyone can pull their knickers back up with chins held high and a big finger to the wind gods and office nerds with satellites, bad coffee and even badder weather forecasts it's the *Windrider* family. Good on you guys for not giving up immediately and making a go for it. What a chapter in your lives! Best of luck and circumstance! Wish we could just race off and come over to act like we're helping, but really just there to remind Andrew we told you so … it's a shitty time of year to go that way! (knock on wood!!!)

Really, hope all comes together. We'll keep our ears open for sailboats passing through that area and let them know you could use transport of goodies. Keep us in the loop.

hugs - J, V & Keemo

TWENTY-ONE

FALL-OUT

Everything seemed different after Chofung's death. The sadness we all felt was almost like a grief, in that there was nothing that would change what had occurred, and nothing that would take back the words and actions of that day.

I put my top back on as I was thoroughly disgusted with this culture and wanted nothing to do with it. It's still on.

The practice of Mogmogians butchering dogs for their meat is not cultural. It began 12 years ago, and many islanders are against it. Still, the fall-out from Sunday has been overwhelming.

On Monday, the island was eerily quiet. In fact, it's been like that all week, and it's Thursday today. No one has spoken to us, and we've spoken to no one.

We did speak with Janet at the Australian Embassy, and she said that the Australian ambassador to the Federal States of Micronesia was meeting with the heads of state in Yap and would bring the incident up during their meeting. Yes! Progress!

Juanito asked to see us. I found myself dreading that meeting. He has done so much for us, and I have developed a real affection and respect for him, as have Andrew and the girls.

When we got to his house, the atmosphere was extremely polite. Yuk! For a while, we talked about nothing in particular, and then he told us he had spent his day going to each house, asking everyone to leave us alone and to respect our opinions and cultures as being different to their own.

Next he asked me to apologise to Falalai for my outburst. I calmly refused. I said very quietly that I had no regret for what I had said and done, and that I would do the same again in a heartbeat. He inclined his head and accepted my position.

Then he said he was extremely upset because he had heard from the chief of police in Yap, who told him we had stated that Juanito had threatened us.

Oh, shit. What had happened?

Apparently, the ambassador had spoken to the heads of state, who had spoken to the chief of police, who had called Juanito, and by the time the message had 'Chinese whispered' its way down the line, somehow it had morphed into an allegation that Juanito had threatened us.

This was bad, really bad. We are here only because Juanito has conveyed to his people that we are his guests. If he was to take away that gesture of goodwill, and ask us to leave, we would have to do so. We were horrified that he could think we would say that about him. His opinion of us must be abysmal.

We told him the truth, and assured him we would be in contact with the embassy first thing in the morning to put things right.

He wished us a quiet and reserved goodnight. It felt like being dismissed by the principal.

We wandered back to *Windrider* so I could retrieve our emails. There was a very enthusiastic one from a Hannah who wanted to come to Mogmog this week and film life here. Awful timing or what! This had come as a result of the *Sydney Morning Herald* article.

Early the next morning, Juanito paid me a visit and passed on a phone message. Somebody named Vincent had contacted Juanito, given him his phone number and wanted me to ring him back. Juanito asked why I needed to call him. I'd never heard of a Vincent, and when I told Juanito this, he was surprised. He said that Vincent was from Wolleiai and owned the store there.

Maybe a box of groceries got there by mistake? Maybe a boat was on its way? Finally, Juanito said it was in relation to the media.

Uh, oh.

Out it came then. An Australian film crew was on its way here, and they were liaising with Vincent in Yap. The story going around was that they had been in contact with us.

Yes! But at 10pm the previous night! And I hadn't even replied yet! I tried to explain that to Juanito, but realised instantly that this was starting to sound pretty hollow. I sounded defensive and my words implausible.

I said that I didn't think it was a good idea to have more Aussies stomping around the island at this stage; we had upset the people of Mogmog enough without that. When I asked Juanito what he thought, he said it was up to me. It was my choice. Gee, thanks! Then and there, I decided that it would not be good.

I hurried to the boat and started ringing. I got hold of Janet at the embassy and told her what Juanito said. She was very concerned and said she would get onto it straight away. Next I rang the Hannah lady, and said that now was not the right time. We talked at length, and she started becoming a little pushy in trying to pin down when they could come. She wanted to ring Juanito and call me for more interviews. It was all a bit much.

Janet rang back. She had just been in touch with the ambassador, who had spoken to the chief of police, who assured him he had said nothing about Juanito making threats. Great!

I asked Janet what she thought about the media situation that was developing, and she agreed with me that it would be best to hold off on visits. It was good to have that second opinion. I'd scarcely replaced the phone when it rang again; Paul was on the line from Perth with the news that *60 Minutes* wanted to come out and film the place.

At about that point, because I'm slow, it hit me that of course Juanito was going to think we had cooked all this up after Sunday. Oh, no!

I rang Janet again and told her my new concern. She said she would phone Juanito and explain the whole situation, making it clear to him that we had nothing to do with the media turning up.

With heart in mouth, I wandered up to speak to the man. He invited me in, and I explained what had transpired that morning and my concern that he must think we concocted all of this. He didn't deny it. When I said I had told the media no, not to come to Mogmog at this time, the relief on his face was palpable. So I asked him why he hadn't said what he wanted in the first place. He smiled. He had just given me the rope to hang myself with. Not that he said that.

He hated the media, he said, and felt that the media would just twist things to say whatever they wanted. Not going to disagree with him on that one! He then stated very quietly that he wanted no media here … ever. Fine by me!

I told him about the chief of police and Janet's call. When I left, I felt the day had taken a turn for the better.

That night, Andrew and I dropped around to Juanito's place as usual, and Andrew gave him $60 for the community to use for fuel to do a community fish. Great idea that. It broke the ice immediately.

Then Juanito told us the party line about Chofung. The dog had bitten three people, and on Mogmog, if a dog bites someone, it is destroyed. No negotiation. The dog is destroyed by the person who was bitten or a member of their family, whenever that person chooses, without telling the dog's owners. Falalai's family did not eat the dog.

Bullshit! I said to Juanito that that was not what had been conveyed at the time or since, and he said that nevertheless, that was what happened, should anybody ask. Weird, though, that there are no old female dogs on the island. It occurred to me that this is in fact a form of contraception. There are old male dogs, but all the females are killed after giving birth.

He also explained that to apologise in this culture is merely an overture to making things right at some time in the future … maybe. It is not an admission of regret, sorrow or wrongdoing. I said I would think about it. I'm still thinking.

At the end of the night, I told Juanito that I held him in the greatest respect and that I was saddened by what this might have done to our friendship. He looked me in the eye and said we would be friends for as long as he breathed. I noticed that that bloody lump in my throat was back.

TWENTY-TWO

GETTING THE COLD SHOULDER

Since I last wrote, things have undergone a subtle but distinct change. It has manifested itself in a number of ways that if taken in isolation would not mean anything but together they become undeniable.

No kids come here any more. A couple of weeks ago, we would have been tearing our hair out trying to get schoolwork done, while politely saying that the kids could play as soon as we had finished our work. Now there is silence in the house. This became a particular problem 10 days ago, when the school year finished for the summer holidays. Until then we had had breaks when the kids were at school.

Not even Persley comes over any more, although there are lots of reasons for that besides this stand-off over how dogs are treated. Andrew had had to talk to Edward, Persley's father, about Persley hanging around the boat. Andrew's concerns were purely to do with safety: the boat is not completely safe, and the thought of it falling on Persley — or anyone else — doesn't bear thinking of. Also, Andrew is now working with resins and potentially dangerous hand-tools. Just last week, Persley's smiling face appeared in the engine hole of the hull while Andrew was resining around the engine bay and resin was falling out of the hole. If that resin had fallen into Persley's eyes, he would likely have been blinded.

Normally, though, Andrew having a word with his father wouldn't deter Persley from bringing his smiling face over here.

The only kid who has been here this week has been rude, bossy Jarrod, strangely enough. He has come a couple of times to play with the puppies that hang around here now. He has been polite at all times. Work that one out.

So now the girls are lonely. For company they have only each other and their busy parents. They fill their days: there's always schoolwork, and Shan has been learning the flute — and doing very well too, says the biased mother — and Diana plays piano. This has been a passion of hers since she was four. We've always thought she may pursue a career in that direction somehow. There's a professional keyboard on the boat that has survived everything, but she no longer goes down there to play.

Both of them have lost their stuffing somehow. They go to the beach with boogie boards but they're alone. It's not that they miss anyone in particular, it's not that they believe they are losing good friends, because they are well aware that these kids only want to be around for the toys, but the loneliness is not something they are used to.

Yesterday I read an email that Diana had written to one of her friends at home. She said that she climbs a particular coconut tree each day; it's near the boat and sort of hangs over it. Up there, she makes things to decorate the tree, to make it pretty so she has somewhere nice to go where no one else can find her. She's up that coconut tree a lot. She's asked Shan to come up, but her sister isn't comfortable up that high, so that means more loneliness.

They are wanting to spend a lot more time with us — not that that wasn't happening before! — and we have started playing cards at night. Andrew and I aren't big card players, so it's been a bit of an education.

* * *

Three of Chofung's pups have taken up residence at our place. Colonel belongs to Jarrod's family, and Arvi and Pepsi belong to Romeo's family. We took them back home umpteen times, but they kept ending up here and they don't even go home at night any more. The girls love them and smother them with attention, but that's a bad thing. They're not our dogs. We don't let them in the house. But now no one else is feeding Arvi and Pepsi, so what do you do?

Dogs here are put up with. They are definitely not man's best friend. When dogs were introduced here 100ish years ago, there was no word in the local language for 'dog'. So the people came up with 'bis', which is the word for trash. This is deliberate. This is the way the locals think of the dogs. Mostly that's because the dogs eat human faeces. But in the dogs' defence, they are not fed as you and I would feed a dog; they must fend for themselves.

Did I mention that there are only six toilets on the island? People go down to the beach, defecate, wipe themselves with a suitable bit of coral and their work is done. The poor starving dogs then go down and clean up after them. The locals act with revulsion if anyone shows affection to a dog. When our neighbours see our house with three pups in residence — as well as Rolande's three from next door, who come to play — I can see why their opinion of us must be one of abhorrence.

Pepsi has already been designated as dinner. As the only female, she will be allowed to have one litter and then she will be killed and eaten. The family has told us this.

Wondering if it would be possible to rescue Pepsi from this fate, I put a call in to the Australian Quarantine and Inspection Service office in Darwin this week. Australia will allow dogs in from Micronesia. It would cost about $2500 for vet bills, and the animal would need to spend 60 days in quarantine, and various other bits and pieces. So we could save Pepsi.

I have been working on Andrew on this one. He's not keen. The last dog we had, our beloved Molly, came to us as an abused refugee at 18 months old. She was a skittish, scrawny, defensive Rottweiler named Jash — after her owners, Jason and Shazza. Against Andrew's wishes at the time, she became Molly, the much-loved dog who ended up with all the bones in the street.

She had a wonderful nature and was loved by all. Sadly, she passed away of natural causes at the age of 14, just before we left. Otherwise she would have been with us on this trip … I digress.

Andrew is no stranger to his wife saving every stray that comes along. He knows another Molly when he sees her. Already he has pointed out the pitfalls of us adopting Pepsi without me even raising the subject; a sure sign he sees the writing on the wall. But then he suggested I ring Palau quarantine to see if we can get her into there at least. Aha! Gotcha! Spotted Andrew and Pepsi smooching yesterday too. Ha!

I have never stolen anything in my life but I am prepared to steal that dog if Romeo's people won't sell her to us. The girls don't know we're thinking of this; mustn't tell them!

* * *

Last week, Yvonne, who lives behind us, was up late with friends laughing quietly, so we went to say hi. Turns out she was drinking a local brew made from yeast and sugar. Try making this at home:

In a large container, place 9 tablespoons of yeast, 19 tablespoons of sugar and a gallon of water. Mix together and leave to stand for 24 hours. You end up with a hot, reasonably potent brew that when chilled and served with a squeeze of lime or lemon is more or less drinkable.

When the girls and I turned up, Yvonne was sitting in darkness, and whenever anyone came past, she and her guests all fell silent, as no one could know they were drinking. We built up a bit of women's solidarity and pledged to make some 'water', so we could host the odd evening too. All good.

But that was before the Chofung incident. Later, when Yvonne asked if we had any 'water', I didn't. I said I'd make some for the following night, and we made a plan to meet. I did as I had said, but when I went to her place, Yvonne wasn't there. The next morning she came over and apologised. No problem. She suggested that we try again for that night. Sure. So she came by, got a huge glass to share with her friends and left.

* * *

Juanito dropped in on Friday morning and asked to see the newspaper and email articles that Paul had sent us. We gave them to him, and he went on his way. Why did he want them and why did he want them now? Over the day, we stewed on those questions.

The high school graduation ceremony was taking place in Falalop that day, and we noted that Juanito didn't go, although we'd expected he would. Very strange ... very strange.

At about 5pm, I popped over to his house to say hi and to let him know that we wouldn't be turning up later that evening for our customary drink, as Shan had requested the inaugural family card night. He started talking about the emphasis on turtle eating in the articles. Intentionally very non-committal, not wanting to cause dissension, I observed that it probably made good press. He talked about practices elsewhere in the world, and then mid-sentence he summarily dismissed me, and added that I could get some bananas on the way out. I felt like that schoolkid again. I don't get it.

The next time we saw Juanito, everything was very polite and nice. The sense of mischief and fun is no longer there. Our conversation is an exchange of information. It is just not the same.

* * *

For everyone on Mogmog, a few things are going badly wrong right now; the island ran out of money this week. The shop here runs on credit. This means that if you don't have money, you run up a tab. If you have a cheque, you can exchange it at the store for credit, rather than cash. The shop will also cash cheques, or did until they ran out of money.

Up until recently, people were coming and asking us to cash cheques. This is something we realised the hard way that we can't allow ourselves to do, as we have no way of recouping the money. People used to come to us for all sorts of things: from coffee, to cloves, to shirts, to nails, to rivets … it was a constant stream. We used to go to bed waiting for the knock on the door for whatever it might be — usually medicines at that time of night. Not any more. No one comes near us; not even Mike and Glen, who had become friends — or so I thought.

At the moment, the store has no means of paying for supplies off the next ship and now — in a stable and horse story — the store is refusing to give credit. No one can get a thing. This is all making people very angry. As it is school holidays, even the teachers don't have money as only a couple of them get holiday pay. As we discussed the situation with Juanito last night, he showed signs of bitterness — the first time I have seen this from him.

* * *

I spent yesterday morning painting the house. *Why?* Bloody good question. It was last painted during the war, I kid you not, and it is dismal, dark and depressing. We are paying no rent, other than all the stuff that keeps wandering out the door as gifts to the greater cause, so I figured I would leave the place better than the way we found it. I bought the paint and eventually got the brushes and rollers, and have been progressing at the rate of 4 litres a week. The place looks a heap better, even though it's a boring white. But that beats concrete grey with a haphazard, as in patchy, coat of green.

As I was working, it struck me that no one would ever know or care whether or not the painting was done. Indeed, Juanito called in to borrow a book and get some coffee and he didn't notice a thing.

Reflecting now on this last week since Chofung died, I think there has been a deterioration in respect on both sides. Clearly, Juanito has lost respect for us, and we have lost respect for large chunks of Mogmogian culture. Since we got here, I have always been the one saying, 'Well, hey, they have nothing, of course they steal; they have to feed their families,' but I no longer feel that way.

These people are almost all overweight, and a lot are obese. Food is not the issue; it's simply that people on Mogmog are lazy. They lie around for much of every day in hammocks, but they complain about what they don't have. The mentality is that they have asked for it, so they should have received it. But let's look at why they haven't received it. Very few of the locals get up and do anything about their lot. There is a demand for copra here, but only a handful of people supply it when the ship comes. There is a demand for bats in Yap, and there are bats in abundance here, but no one thinks about supplying the demand. There is money to be made from tourism, if anyone really tried. Businesses in Yap want to buy lavalavas for the tourist trade, but only one woman on Mogmog is making them.

This attitude of lying around and complaining that no one sends you anything, coupled with the events of the last week, has eroded my respect. I fully believe that Juanito has his list of quibbles with us, the blow-ins. After all, we fraternise with the filthy *bis*. Even so, I wouldn't apologise and no longer will I go topless to fit in with local practices.

I no longer feel that Juanito is supporting us out of friendship. I feel now that he is tolerating us, looking forward to our departure, and to us leaving behind a whole heap of timber and glass, so he can build the verandah he's been talking about. I also feel that if the embassy and the ambassador weren't vocally involved in this, our safety might be in question, particularly if Juanito should need to leave for any reason.

TWENTY-THREE

HARD YARDS

Can you believe we have put in a small vegie garden? Using seeds from fresh vegies we brought here as well as packet seeds, we have planted pumpkins — feeling queasy? — tomatoes, peas, beans and lettuces. So far we have harvested one Chinese long bean. Admittedly, it's underwhelming as returns go, but hey, it's a start. To save our vegie patch from the chickens, puppies, toads and kids, we've fenced it in, and it looks like it will be ready for harvest as we leave.

Curious, we asked Juanito why no one on Mogmog grows vegies. When he said it was because the chickens eat the plants, we asked why they don't put the chickens in runs so they can have vegies and find the eggs. His answer was that chickens in a run are easy to catch, so they would be stolen.

* * *

The repairs to the boat are progressing nicely, which is just as well given that things are so tense here. Amos delivered the resins and glass last week, so we were able to reschedule the repairs and ramp things up a bit. As you know, the wooden hull structure has been in place for a while. Andrew resined the entire hull, making it waterproof. With that massive job out of the way, he could start work on the inside. First off, he removed the floor on the starboard side, which was buckled and battered. Next, he reinstalled the two water tanks on that side, complete with baffles. To get at the hull, he had to partially remove the kitchen. Then he laid two layers of glass inside the hull, which is now waterproof and ready to receive both water and fuel. The aft floor area in the engine bay area has also been glassed. Andrew seated the engine pod in place and resined it, so it's ready for the engine to go in.

Currently, he's putting down the floor structure and replacing the access points for the fuel and water tanks. After this the floor will be glassed into place, and that will be the end of internal glass repairs.

Next week, the starboard engine will be returned to its home, then Andrew will give the outside of the same hull two layers of glass. Once a few holes in the port hull are filled and glassed, that will be the end of the glassing. Yay! Then on to a heap of other major repairs and installations, of course.

Replacing the port engine will be a big job, and then Andrew will need to spend about a week rewiring and replumbing. Once he instals the new watermaker pumps, the reverse osmosis system can be up and running again. He'll also have to put in two new inverters to get the power systems back up. What a step forward that will be.

The hull will need to be fared to make it smooth. This is a bugger of a job, involving many days of sanding with an aptly named torture board — a long board covered in sandpaper. Following that, we prime the hulls and antifoul them.

Then, just when the end is in sight, comes the biggest challenge of this whole venture. The boat is sitting so that the back of the hulls are about at the high-water mark. If you picture a catamaran hull as having a top part and a bottom part, the bottom of the hulls is 5ish feet in depth. The low-water mark sits below that, a sharp 2-foot drop. Then comes a gradual decline to the waterline. The final hurdle is a tabletop reef which is exposed at low tide. This extends out for about 40 metres.

How are we going to get the boat into the deep water on the other side of this reef? This has been the topic of many late-night discussions. Do we involve the locals? After last week: no, we do not.

We think we have sussed out a way to do it alone. Andrew has designed a frame to be made out of 1000 feet of timber: quite a requirement. Each hull is to be cradled. Then there is a base for the rudders and beaching keels to sit in. The cradles are joined by crossbeams. At the bottom of the base, there will be crossbeams shaped like stocks. Where the head would go, will be two rows of four 44-gallon drums. All of this will be placed in a wooden luge track, in three pieces. As the boat moves down, the last part of the track will become the first, and so on. To stop it running away on us, the boat will be shackled to trees, using the block and tackle.

Well before we carry out this exercise, we'll set up a mooring beyond the reef. The plan is to launch *Windrider* at low tide, as we don't want her to be thumping around on the reef. It would be better to get her out to the edge of the deep before winching her off onto the mooring. We'll leave the drums in place as we float off the edge with the tide. Sound easy? No … didn't think so.

Through the Australian Embassy in Pohnpei, we enquired about the chance that the US Navy might be able to help us off, as they have a large presence in this region and they are always coming and going. The answer we got back was that we would need to relinquish ownership of *Windie* to the Federated States of Micronesia. Only then, if they so choose, the FSM Government can request assistance from the US Navy, who will consider it at that point.

* * *

I am very conscious, as I reread this, that it comes across as a tale of life on Mogmog, with the people of Mogmog. To put everything in perspective, Andrew is working approximately 13-hour days, at least six days a week. We hope to be out of here in five weeks, which is probably optimistic but we're sticking to that goal at this stage. Five weeks from now, Andrew will have spent some 1200 hours working on the boat while on this island.

We have no scales, but I would estimate that Andrew has lost 10 kilograms. He is borderline depressed, and I battle to get him to eat. Val sent multivitamins — thank goodness he takes those. His hands and feet are never free of cuts, and in this weather, they don't heal well. They all get infected, even though we are constantly slathering on Bactroban antibiotic cream and covering it all up with Elastoplast, every cut generates pus for about two weeks. Since our arrival, he hasn't been without infections. He battles diarrhoea on a daily basis. As I have said before, any emotional or mental stress always affects Andrew physically. On the odd occasion that we have argued over the years, it has always been intensely emotional, and this has always led to a physical decline. I am watching this happen to him now.

When we first arrived, he was at his worst. To my relief he slowly and steadily picked up, but the events of the last little while have sent him downhill fast. Also, as he is doing manual work, he has time to mull things over, which is not always a positive. Now that he has nutted out a plan for getting the boat over the reef, he has started thinking a lot about what is going on here, and perhaps reading more into comments made than was intended. Obviously, I am guilty of that too. But Andrew has that tendency to hyperfocus on issues, to the point where he won't sleep, which then exacerbates his physical problems.

I hate this cycle, but there's no quick fix. Only getting out of here will put an end to it. We all try to pep each other up, and realise that we are all getting grumpy and tired.

Last night we watched some old episodes of *Get Smart*, and that was great. Pure, dumb, happy escapism.

On a lighter note, guess what? Andrew and I are going to try to keep Pepsi! I knew I'd win that one. So now, *if* we can take her into Palau, and *if* we can fly her home or have her accepted into the next country without it upsetting Australian customs, and *if* we can con someone into looking after her until we get home or at least back to Australia, and *if* we can convince her Mogmogian family to part with her, then we can have her.

Haven't told the kids yet, but I'm onto it right now!

TWENTY-FOUR

IN THE DOLDRUMS

As I write, I'm really not having a good day. I'm feeling very flat and have a headache that I can't shake.

Yesterday, I started my day by ringing the shipping people in Yap. The supply ship had been at Mogmog on the weekend. It had left Yap and done a circuit of all the Yap State outer islands, with the first and last stop being here at Ulithi Atoll. By the time it got back to us, it was overloaded big time and couldn't take anyone to Yap. On top of causing a lot of inconvenience, it meant that the teachers couldn't get away for their holidays and medical cases couldn't get out, which seemed wrong. The general feeling was that there would have to be a wedgie run, just to Ulithi — a round trip of 180 nautical miles — before the next scheduled trip, which is in 12 days' time.

Juanito asked me to try to find out what I could, hence the phone call. No, there's not going to be a wedgie ship trip. When I wandered over to Juanito's house to let him know this, he was quite subdued, and there was no cheery wave and hello, as there used to be.

He appeared in my doorway a little later, asking for lead solder from Andrew. By then Andrew had dashed off to Falalop in the dinghy, to drop off the other rudder to Amos and check the mail. He had also been asked to chase up an envelope filled with phone recharge cards that was supposed to have arrived for Juanito some weeks earlier.

Andrew returned bearing the long-awaited guitar strings. The envelope of cards, he'd discovered, had been given to Aiden, Juanito's son, the previous Friday last week.

We found the solder, and went to report in with Juanito. The guitar strings were received with thanks. When we told Juanito about the envelope, he said that he knew about it and had it already. Somewhat offhandedly, he wanted to know where the solder was. In fact we had already dropped it off with Raymond so that he could repair Juanito's coffee percolator, so that Juanito could drink the coffee we'd given him on Sunday. Finding Juanito quite dismissive, we quickly made our goodbyes, leaving him settling back into his hammock to read the book we'd loaned him.

Then came the good part of the day. I got on the phone and found out that we can take a dog to Palau as long as it is under 12 weeks of age. If it's over 12 weeks, it must have a vaccination certificate for rabies. Fat chance of getting that around here. The vet I spoke to was lovely. His name is Minhea and he is writing a letter for us to give to quarantine in Palau stating that he will vaccinate Pepsi, and that under international law she can come into Palau as she is under 12 weeks old. He was really pleased and encouraging, and we talked more about getting her back to Perth. His advice was that we should fly her home from Palau, as if she goes into Indonesia — or most of the South Pacific areas — Australian quarantine will not allow her into Australia.

Fantastic news! Minhea said not to ask the Palauan officials about bringing her, as they may say no, but just to rock up with her, with his letter, and he would take responsibility. What a nice guy!

* * *

My high spirits quickly evaporated after Andrew handed me an envelope from Amos with a statement of where we are at with our 'kitty'. I opened it without much thought and then read … and reread. Originally we had been quoted 72 cents per pound for freight. According to the statement in my hands, we had been charged at 95 cents per pound — there is an island charge and an off-island charge, and the off-island is of course higher, which is where we'd been hit. To add insult to injury, oversize items incurred a higher rate again, namely $2 a pound. Taking all this into account meant the stuff Amos had brought out last Monday cost US$800. Yet we'd paid just $1.50 a pound for the identical freight from Brisbane to Palau with Pacific Flier! Andrew pointed all this out to Amos at Falalop, but he shrugged and smiled. This meant our kitty was gone in one fell swoop.

Each time we need more funds, my mum goes out to the post office and parts with her own money (until I can get things organised to pay her back), then rings me with the number, which I forward on to the relevant person. Although this might sound easy, Mum is nearly 80 and suffers badly from Obsessive Compulsive Disorder. This makes doing anything a major drama for her. It pains me that now I'll have to ask her to go and do yet another one of these transactions. She never complains, and does whatever I ask, whenever I ask it, so I hate to ask her again.

* * *

Later in the day we had a visit from Catherine, the Peace Corps worker. She had brought us a gift: a pack of scorched almonds from her trip to Yap. That was so thoughtful!

Inevitably, our conversation led to the events of the Sunday when Chofung died and the fall-out since. Catherine's response was surprising and we pressed her to enlighten us more. In her view, the local people had shown deference to us, because they had not carried out their usual practice of taking the dog's head and shafting it onto a tree until it becomes a skeleton. A fortnight after her arrival, she told us, two young boys had killed two dogs as part of a graduation ceremony. They had then put the heads on display until eventually they were eaten clean.

The barbarity sickened me! What Catherine told me confirmed that these people are everything I have been trying to deny to myself. Another chunk of my respect evaporated.

Catherine went on to explain her understanding of the villagers' view of us — in general and in relation to that awful day. Her first point was that they have no acceptance of having stolen any of our stuff. On Mogmog, if someone has something, and someone else thinks they need it more, they just take it. As Catherine sees it, the people resent us because we did not give them everything we had. They simply got what they could.

For a woman to yell at a man is the highest level of disrespect on Mogmog. To then not apologise means a total loss of face for the man. So any man I have shouted at — how many have there been, I wonder — automatically loathes us. Catherine says the younger men all want us gone. A few of the respected middle-aged men have told them to back off.

Another black mark against us is that we have made such an issue about what is deemed to be a private matter, namely Chofung, and that is regarded as unconscionable.

And so the list of black marks went on. Basically we are scum — filthy, dog-loving scum that no one wants here — and no one wants to have anything to do with us. As to why it went so wrong, apparently I should have gone to the women and asked to learn to weave, cook and be part of their lives, not part of my husband's. I chose not to; I thought I would be intruding. In my defence, I offered to help at the school a number of times, and eventually gave up. They didn't want me there.

So where does that leave us? Here's how I would sum up our situation. On the one hand we should be giving the islanders everything they ask for — and we have — because that is their culture. But at the same time, it's insulting to give them everything, because it looks like we are throwing money at a problem, which is patronising. Also, the people would prefer us to spend time learning their culture.

Talk about having your cake and eating it too! I have spent about $4000 replacing stolen items that are essential to us. Each time I put in a shopping list, I order a heap more than we need. And before we place an order, we always ask people what they need and get stuff for them. Andrew spent perhaps 50 hours making the ham-smoker and donated all the materials. If only we were made of money! We are a normal, average Aussie family. And when am I going to get time to learn to weave and to make bread? I could fit it in between 2 and 4am maybe! And even if all the time the locals loathe us, they still come knocking, wanting more. So far today I've handed out yeast, onions, chilli, pepper and cloves. One day we even gave shirts to Antoinette: she was about to go to some other islands, where they wear shirts, and she didn't have one. Isn't that a parent's responsibility?

Mindful that we will go eventually, Juanito has already earmarked the chairs we bought — while we're still sitting on them.

I'm sorry, but I've had enough of the hypocrisy. Every day I hear people say 'But we don't have', and then the same people lie in hammocks for hours on end — and come and get stuff from us.

As for all the media crap, apparently it's been said that we have orchestrated and manipulated all of that, and are using it to threaten them. It seems to me that Juanito is doing his best to control us.

By the time Catherine left, I was furious. Quiet and furious.

Andrew and I decided we had better do our usual ritual around Juanito, so off we went. When we arrived, Aiden and James were there. The last time I'd seen Aiden, I had spent the better part of the day writing his application for a New Zealand uni scholarship. I often tell people that I bluffed my way through uni, and earned an A-plus in bullshit 101. I write pretty good crap, and if I say so myself, this application was great.

Andrew asked Aiden if he had put in the application, and he said yes … no, thank you. When Andrew tried to explain to James what I had done, Juanito cut in and changed the subject.

Aiden made a point of telling Andrew that he must go to the men's house each time he goes to Falalop to state his business. If he doesn't, the men there will exercise their right to take and keep our dinghy. I stifled my seething. Andrew smiled and said, 'No problems.'

I asked if there was any further news on the ship. Apparently not.

Then we all fell into silence — uncomfortable silence. I have never felt so unwelcome. Then it clicked. Ellie had been relegated to the back table, rather than being part of the conversation as she normally would be, and the other women were cooking. It was me who was the problem. I was sitting in a circle of men and expecting to be part of the conversation. I felt humiliated and furious.

Making 'I've got to cook' excuses, I left with Chook, urging Andrew to stay. Night had fallen, and I walked back to the house with tears rolling down my face. I cooked in silence, and the girls made me beautiful cheer-up cards. Andrew was back within half an hour, and we sat outside in the darkness and talked.

I'm clear about my position. I'm not going back to that house. I won't go where I am not welcome. I will be polite. I will give whatever is asked of me. And I refuse to be treated like shit and regarded as shit by people with values such that they will proudly display a severed dog's head. By people who take, take, take, take, and if they can't take they steal. By people who destroy things and don't own up to it. By people who take pride in causing destruction because it stops others from having enjoyment. I'm having a hard time not thinking of these people as barbaric, dangerous natives. They killed a missionary here in the 1940s. It's not that long ago.

Woke up this morning feeling flat. Walked onto the boat to do emails on the HF radio, and Andrew was playing Dr Hook. The song was 'Years from now'. Listen to the words sometime. They undid me.

TWENTY-FIVE

SHIPPING NEWS

There are two ships which service the outer Yapese islands. There is the state ship, which originates from Yap and does a slow loop — as in about six weeks for the round trip — of all the outer islands. It has an accommodation section aft. Midships it has a central flat area covered with a tarp, where for $12 you can sit and get passage one way: to wherever, from wherever. This is also where all the goods are stowed. This is where people sit and some have a great old time getting plastered on everyone else's plonk. This ship hits us twice in the loop, as we are the first point out and the last point in. Currently, it has no refrigeration — yes, still — and that has been the case for the last seven weeks.

Now the hydraulics have packed up, so there is no lifting capacity from the hold area, which is below, in the bow. It is here that the stores keep their stock so that it's away from the hungry hordes. You'll also find construction equipment and the odd car. This ship is currently due for service and will be pulled out of the water after the next trip.

The other ship is the *Caroline Voyager*, which originates out of Pohnpei and travels through all points to Yap and back. The round trip takes about eight weeks. The *Caroline Voyager* is structured very much the same as the state ship. It is scheduled to be drydocked for regular maintenance next time it hits Pohnpei.

The idea is that the two ships pass each other so that we see one or other of them about once every six weeks. Clearly, given that the schedules don't match up, this is not going to work. Nothing about them is coordinated: what genius decided that both will be out of the water indefinitely at the same time! After the next planned ship, neither ship is posting a schedule until they are back in the water. Apparently this has happened before, and one time, these islands had no ship for over a year.

As of now, there is no rice, sugar or staple of any other kind on the whole atoll. Forget Mogmog, the whole atoll. And forget luxuries like toilet paper, mozzie coils, soap and the like. Oh, and by the way, no stores will stock feminine sanitary items. They are offensive. So the women here rely on their friends and family in Yap to send these items on the now non-existent ships. What are they supposed to use now that that supply has fallen through? Leaves?

Falalop prides itself on having wifi access from as far away as the anchorage. That has been down for over a month, and there are no plans to fix it. There goes banking etc.

To add to this list of hassles, the power is run from Yap. Each island has its own generator. You pay through Yap State to get a code that you plug into your meter, which then allows so many units of power to be accessed. The computer crashed a week ago. Consequently no one can top up their power. Over a week ago we paid to get power to the women's house, because Andrew is using power from there as it is close to the boat. Since the power ran out there, we have had leads going the 200 metres from the house to the boat. We are down to 28 units now, and there is no indication of when the computer will be fixed.

People are already starting to use generator sets. Don't you love the dulcet tones of the genny as you peacefully sleep with all the other stuff that squawks, yaps, barks, clangs, shuffles, clonks and crows around here? And of course running generators then puts strain on the fuel supplies, which are dwindling fast.

So to recap, we have run out of all food stocks at the store, we're running low on fuel and power, there's no internet at Falalop and no one can tell us when a ship might come.

There is an upside to all of this. It became obvious when we went to Juanito's last night — yes, I've caved in already. He has way too much on his mind to worry about us and what some airy-fairy media somebody might be saying in another hemisphere. I think reality is winning over hypotheticals here, and I'm very glad.

* * *

Operation pooch rescue is very much underway. I received an email from Minhea, the vet in Palau. He has put together a plan that will not upset Palauan officials. When we arrive, either he or someone else will meet us, and we'll go and buy a cage, visit quarantine, and then all of us will go to Minhea's office to do the vaccinations and health report.

Our next step was to find a temporary home for Moggie, the doggie from Mogmog. She will need somewhere to live before we get back to Australia. I asked a few family members and, for varying reasons, they are unable to take her. So I sent out a general email to our scaly mates. The emails went nuts. Within a minute we had a firm offer.

Then one of Diana's best mates wrote saying that she was busting to have her, but had to convince her parents. Lea and John are great people. John is a seaman who troubleshoots all over the world, so is mostly away from home. They have three kids. Kirsty is in the middle. They also have Bonny and Clyde, the two tabby cats, and a beautiful garden. Next day I received an ecstatic email from Kirsty saying her parents said *yes*!

I rang and spoke to Lea, and she convinced me she was happy with the arrangement, as was John. Apparently he replied by email in under a minute with one word, 'Yes!', as the reply. Moggie is sorted!

Despite this exciting news, we still haven't told the girls. I am so scared that the locals will kill these pups just to spite us. And they would. Last night, when I was lying in bed, I heard an air-rifle being shot about 20 metres from our window. It made me realise how vulnerable these pups are. I'm not sure we're going to be able to keep our plans secret all the way through. I can't wait to tell Shan and Diana!

Moggie looks like a helicopter about to take off every time we go near her. I've never seen a tail rotate so fast.

* * *

Andrew went to Falalop with Shan this morning to get much-needed hardware supplies and money. They'd hoped also to come back with an inverter, but unfortunately this seems to be bogged in Guam.

Amos greeted them with the news that the ship has been delayed until 30th June. That could be tricky; we don't have enough food to get us to 30th June. Ten or so days ago, we ran out of alcohol of the bought variety.

Without the ship, it looks like we're stymied. We have all things timber, hardware and chandlery coming on it, and the plan was to have the hulls ready for antifoul when the ship got here, with a view to leaving by about 30th June. So much for that.

On the bright side, we have a few options. If a sufficiently large number of people jump up and down loudly enough, the powers that be may reconsider, particularly if the store owners need stock — even though we all know the store owners have no money to buy stock. Alternatively, we might be able to get together a group and charter a boat from Yap. Fishermen are sometimes happy to come out here if their diesel is paid for. But again, that would need the store owners to be in on it.

We did have 100 kilograms of rice in our order for the community, so perhaps Juanito will use his influence to get the ship happening.

Or I could fly to Yap with Amos and spend the weekend there, getting everything, and flying it all back, which will cost about half the price of buying the plane!

* * *

They say that every cloud has a silver lining. Now that the ship is not arriving when it should, Andrew is taking the opportunity to do some of the things we've never got around to. At the starboard bow, past our bedroom, is the 'everything area'. When we set off from Perth, it was a grey-carpeted space stacked with the gun safe, fishing rods, bedding, inflatable toys, life jackets, fishing gear — in short, everything. Now it is gleaming white and has rod racks and neatly organised shelves. A bit mindboggling really. Andrew might even get to the floors! We have lugged the flooring 4000 miles so far from Perth, so it'd be nice to get there some time! Didn't expect it to be here, though!

* * *

Over the weekend, the two of us have done a lot of thinking, trying to work out how to make the most of this situation, and do the best with the cards we've been dealt. The standoff is unchanged, and I have no intention of apologising to anyone.

I cast my mind back to something that had struck me during our recent travels in Indonesia. A lot of the people we met had a one-step mentality: they lived so much in the present that their focus was 100 per cent on the step they were taking *right now*. As far as I could tell, there was no sense of how current actions might impact on the future.

When we were in Bandaneira, we were contacted by the local fishmonger, who tracked us down because he had crayfish and he wanted a premium price for them; few locals would be interested at that price. We were, and dutifully followed him back to the market to find three large female crays full to the brim with roe. They were dead already, or we would have bought them on the spot and got them back into the water. The fishmonger could not believe we would not accept such crayfish.

Countless times we saw people cleaning their houses by sweeping everything out onto the front doorstep and leaving it there. There you go. House clean!

Countless times we would cart our rubbish to the designated rubbish areas only to see it float past us soon after because locals had ripped the bag apart to see if there was anything good to salvage from it.

We saw people defecating into the water that they then fished in and ate from.

The concept of getting repeat business didn't appear to exist. Stall owners in Ambon would often start bargaining with us at

20 times the local price, and then we would haggle down from there. We always knew we would pay a premium, and didn't mind doing so, but we were not prepared to pay more than 10 times the local going rate. However the transaction ended — perhaps I walked away empty-handed in disgust or having purchased whatever I wanted at a price that was unfair — I never went back. Another trick some vendors tried was to agree on the price, and then 'mistake' the change. Again, thoroughly pissed off, I never gave them my custom a second time.

There was always, however, a Chinese-owned shop in every village. The prices never varied, and neither did the quality. It was slightly more expensive, but unfailingly predictable, so guess where we went to shop.

Andrew and I had often commented that the Mogmogians, although a completely different people, did share elements of this way of thinking. They don't tend to plan or consider the future, and in their day-to-day living they tend to react to the situation in the 'right here and now'.

Taking all of this into account, we devised a plan to improve our poor public relations. Andrew would repair the school principal's traditional canoe. Because it had been disused for years, it is no longer 'traditional', so Andrew is able to fix it without 'detraditionalising' it. We would invite some kids to play with the kids' toys, as if we had never done it before. Diana and Shan went through their clothes and picked out the dresses that no longer fit, ready to give them away. We would walk through the streets and say hi to everyone. We would negotiate to buy Pepsi if at all possible. Andrew would give his not-needed spear gun to Raymond as a gift. We would buy 100 kilograms of rice for the village — for delivery whenever the ship comes.

It was yesterday, a Sunday, when we decided this. Now, at 1pm Monday, we have 10ish kids playing on the Rip Stiks, Raymond has the spear gun, and Pepsi's owners have agreed to let us have her, though we are still negotiating the details through Raymond. We want to pay for her, so we know she is ours. They don't want money.

Things are looking up. Mike came by saying he had a crayfish for us. In return, I gave him a large jar of coffee. Three kids have new dresses. The principal's canoe is all fixed and can be used tomorrow. By a stroke of luck, all the elders of the village were at his place when Andrew was working on the boat.

There is even more good news: we found out that the *Caroline Voyager* will be here today. It's heading off to Yap next and will drop in here again on Saturday to offload cargo, including the 100 kilos of rice for the village and all our stuff. It's then doing a copra run through to Pohnpei. When we found out this last detail, we told as many people as we could, and as I write, the whole island is cutting and processing copra to earn money for the island.

I think this positive approach on our part just might work. Maybe we can turn around our relationship with our Mogmog hosts by acting as though we are starting all over again. I would love to think so. All I can say is that, if it does work, a bit of careful thought goes a long way.

Now if we can sit our girls down later today and introduce them to their own little puppy, who we can take away with the island's blessing, I will be a much happier girl.

TWENTY-SIX

GETTING BACK ON TRACK, SORT OF

Well, last night was full on and happy. The undercover area was full of kids Rip-Stikking in the dark, the fluoro wheels lighting up the night. Kids came from everywhere, and what was surprising was there were no arguments, and the kids were very polite.

On Raymond's sayso, I went to speak to Jackson and Mandy, the owners of Pepsi. They were approachable and lovely, and happily agreed to part with Pepsi. They wanted no money, but when it was offered they looked grateful.

With those negotiations done, Pepsi has become Moggie Doggie Barrie and moved in. So we have three very happy girls in the house and one resignedly happy dad. Moggie reigns supreme in her newfound castle — it took her about 10 seconds to get used to *that* role — and we are busy tipping out the other pups. Start as you mean to go on and all that. They won't be coming with us when we leave, so we don't want them to become too attached.

Mike dropped in again, bringing native apples and a berry named woolieri, which the girls love.

Another visitor was Flage, Juanito's grandson, a thoroughly nice kid of about 15 or 16. What he wanted to discuss was helping me to get back our iPod. We know that Reno, Persley's brother, stole it, and Flage had some advice on the best way to get it back. Although it goes against our principles, we think it would be best just to drop it. Reno's a volatile kid who is already on tuba suspension for violence, so best we let that one go.

As we chatted, what Flage was saying confirmed everything Catherine had told us regarding the feelings of the islanders towards us.

I guess the current situation is that we have a truce. On the surface, the islanders are happy to be friendly, and the giving and receiving has resumed. All is good.

Early in the evening we went to Juanito's for a drink and a chat. Our contribution was some homemade woobla, though we allowed ourselves just one glass each, as we are conscious that we are not supposed to be making the stuff. When we'd finished our drinks, Juanito started refilling Andrew's glass, but not mine. I knew it was because women 'don't drink' so I took it in my stride.

After this happened about four times, Juanito apologised for not filling my glass. I replied that it was fine, and that I understood. Then he laughed, saying that it was pretty silly that he was not allowing me to drink with them when he frequently asked me to order vodka for him on the ship. He laughed again; I smiled silently.

When Andrew suggested soon after that we should go home and cook dinner, Juanito asked if he could send Flage home with me to borrow $10 so he could get Juanito some cigarettes.

I cooked and gave the girls dinner. They played with the puppy and the kids on Rip Stiks. After they went to bed, I sat up reading. Eventually Andrew got home at 11pm, and by then he didn't want dinner. One of Juanito's friends had dropped in, and the chief wouldn't hear of Andrew going until the friend's huge tuba bottle was empty. He felt obliged to stay.

That is now the third and final time that I will allow myself to be summarily 'dismissed' by 'the principal'. Particularly one that I am losing respect for by the day. I can't abide hypocrisy. And this island's culture is firmly based in just that. And it is clearly displayed in the daily actions of the chief.

* * *

So much for the *Caroline Voyager* turning up as promised. It was supposed to call in here, then leave on Sunday, getting to Yap on Monday, where after doing a quick refill it would be back here again by Saturday 19th June. Today is Thursday the 17th and there has been no sign of the ship yet, so if it does turn up prior to going to Yap, it would be back here next Thursday at the earliest. I don't think we have enough food to get that far. We'll get by, but it won't be easy. And what if the ship is delayed again? What happens then?

Last night, Andrew went down to Juanito's without me. Juanito got so smashed he had to be half-carried to bed by the women. This didn't stop him asking us for cough mixture, corned beef and a bar of soap, though. At what point do we start saying no?

At this stage we have food, but not much. We ate all things fresh long ago, and the cupboard looks like it belongs to Old Mother Hubbard. And, hey, we have another mouth to feed now.

Shan has broken out in pigmented blotches; I don't know if they are a reaction to adult multivitamins, as we have no kids' ones, or a reaction to lack of vitamins.

It is now Sunday after Mass. The ship has still not arrived. We have one more meal of fresh meat, chicken niblets, a few dried meals, two cans of 'meal in a can' and one can of tinned ham. There are no more butane cans for the gas burner, so it's the barbeque or the microwave.

Last night I cooked chicken drumsticks in tostada sauce in the microwave, and then crunched them up on the hotplate, using up the last of our butane. The kids wolfed it down, but Andrew wouldn't touch it. Andrew comes from a family where it was commonplace to see a full dinner plate fly through the air and smash against a wall, accompanied by an 'I'm not eating *this shit!*' The legacy of that is that he happily and gratefully eats anything he's served, and thanks you for it every time. But not last night. I knew I was on shaky ground resorting to the microwave, but there was not a lot I could do.

After that, he went to bed at 8pm again. Every night since Monday, he has gone to bed at 8pm, saying he's exhausted. He looks exhausted. He acts exhausted. But this has to be more than that. I'm sure this is the beginning of depression.

Admittedly, the news has not been good lately. We got an email from Dennis in Palau saying the rudder wasn't there yet. In the same bunch of emails, we were cc'ed in one from Randy in Guam to a friend of his, saying he was off sailing and could the friend help us please. The combined effect of these emails, along with the ship not turning up, is taking its toll. If the rudder isn't here soon, we can kiss goodbye to leaving in four weeks and celebrating Andrew's birthday in Palau.

I'm now really concerned about Andrew. He's not sleeping well either. I've seen these early signs of depression in him before, and if they're not checked somehow, he'll be crook in a few days, and the wheels will start to fall off.

* * *

The ship finally made it here later on Sunday and left again in abysmal weather. It is about to head off to Japan for dry-dock. So no quick turnaround there! I rang to find out about the state ship, and was told it will still not be leaving Pohnpei until 30th June. Our food supplies won't stretch that far. I had no choice but to ring Amos and the store in Yap. Sigh.

The store responded to my Monday morning request by putting together a vegie shop for me, and there was no mention of needing money, just 'Hi, Jenny, we'll get it to the airport straight away.' Whoa! I didn't think I was hearing right! I phoned Amos a while later and, sure enough, everything was all assembled, ready for him to fly it across to us. I could *not* believe it, and sent off a quick, heartfelt thank you! to Dominic at the Yap store. I think they finally realise that we are customers, and not bad ones either. What a relief.

But then the weather caved in. When we had phoned Amos, they were having sunny conditions in Yap and he was preparing to leave. On Mogmog we had 8/8ths cloud at less than 1000 feet, wind at 42 knots and visibility of about 600 metres. So we let him know, and the flight was canned. What else could anyone do? Consequently there was no food. It was going to have to be turtle meat.

Having said earlier that I abide hypocrisy, I have a problem with turtle meat: it doesn't come on a polystyrene tray at Coles or Woollies. I have never killed an animal to eat it, yet I love a good steak or roast. For some reason, the thought of turtle turns my stomach. I need to think about why that is the case. It makes no sense. I guess I'm not alone.

Tuesday dawned a little clearer, and Amos was expected to be here by 10am. The relief was really quite overwhelming. It's the little logistic things that can undo you in this sort of situation. It's the lack of being able to take control of a situation. You want to be Jean-Luc Picard of *Star Trek* and 'Make it so', but it just won't be so, no matter how you try to make it so. The old adage that the harder you work, the luckier you work just doesn't cut it on Mogmog. What happens is that you become incredibly grateful for whatever you can get.

And we were. Amos arrived and was met by Diana and Dad.

Three big boxes emerged from the plane: chicken in boxes — that is the most space-effective way to send it, and you get max meat per space. Steak — four packs; frozen vegies — six big packs; mozzie coils; rat traps; and enough yeast and sugar to make an island fall over. Fantastic! No spuds — I really wanted spuds, bugger it! We have food to last till 1st July, when the ship will hopefully finally make it.

* * *

The difference in Andrew has been amazing. At his instigation, 'Operation Boat Clean' started. All us girls were at it, and now the boat is gleaming and is home again. We now have our cuppa down here in the mornings; there's no gas at the house anyway. The other evening we watched a movie here. I came late at night with a torch and it was like seeing for the first time the work we had done. It took me by surprise how beautiful it looks — not because it's flash, coz it ain't, but it's home again!

Today, I have started moving back in to *Windrider*. It'll take time, but we have that. I'm gradually making spaces in the house and filling up hatches here. For the first time, I am writing this sitting on the couch in the boat! Usually, I sit with the computer on my lap, surrounded by one unpainted wall and three painted ones, with perhaps five puppies at the door, and an endless stream of islanders all wanting something. To have peace, quiet and comfort is a real luxury. We're getting there.

Maybe tomorrow, the glass on the hulls? I hope so.

* * *

Today is 28th June; the end of the financial year is in two days. Guess what? The power plant office at Falalop caught fire yesterday. Only the paperwork and computers were destroyed. That's the one and only office on the islands. Coincidence?

TWENTY-SEVEN

NO, NOT *ANOTHER* DELAY!

It's 29th June and the fucking supply ship is not coming! The last ship called in here six weeks ago.

As soon as Amos emailed with that joyful bit of news, I rang the shipping people to check. Sure enough, they are waiting on a part that they hope will arrive in two weeks. And who's going to believe *that*!

Andrew estimates that we have three weeks' work to do once the ship delivers those final materials we need. So *if, if, if* what the shipping people say is true, that means the boat will be here in about three weeks, and we can leave in six weeks. That puts it at mid August. So much for celebrating Andrew's birthday surrounded by friends in Palau.

What's much worse is that Shan's 10th birthday is on 11th August. When her last birthday came around, things weren't super festive for her. It was stinking hot, and we were all alone on a deserted island off West Australia attending to a boat repair. I did make her a double layer cake with choccy icing and lollies all over it, but we pretty much spent the day beaching the boat to bend a rudder back into shape after hitting a rock that didn't exist, according to the charts — both electronic and paper. Even though we had plenty of fun that day, despite the situation, we promised her that her next birthday would be somewhere great, and she could have a really big treat, even a party if she wanted. *Stuffed* if we're going to celebrate her 10th birthday stuck on this island, with no provisions, no cake, no friends and no presents or party. There is *no* way I'm going to let that happen.

Fired up about finding a solution, I have phoned the store on Yap, and Dominic is trying to locate a boat we could charter to deliver our supplies. The problem is the quantity we have. Here's our list: 1000 foot of timber, eight empty avgas 400-gallon drums, assorted hardware items and probably $2000 worth of food and booze.

Straight after the last ship got here, on 18th May, I placed my follow-up order — with the expectation of receiving supplies two weeks later, when the next ship was scheduled. I figured out how much we'd need and then doubled it. Andrew thought I was being stupid. Ha!

At the moment, we have enough food to get us through about a week. We're totally out of butane for the gas burner. Yesterday evening we ran out of one LPG gas cylinder, so are on our last one now. Once that's gone, we won't be able to use the oven, hotplate or hot water on the boat. We are even down to our last lighter.

The obvious thing, as so many friends have pointed out, is that the locals are able to live here, therefore so can we. Fair comment. But it's not that simple. The island is out of fuel, which means there's no fishing except by canoe. Andrew and I need our existing fuel in case we need to motor across to Falalop to pick up deliveries or meet Amos for supplies. In terms of rock fishing, there are no fish near the island; I looked. There are heaps of coconuts.

The Mogmogians all have their own fruit and vegie supplies. Every banana, papaya, pumpkin, taro, rose apple, berry — you name it — is owned. You can't just go and pick something. That's theft. Consequently, our family doesn't have access to any locally grown produce unless someone gives it to us, which does occasionally happen. The shop is closed and empty, and has been for about six weeks.

The people of the island do all their cooking in outdoor kitchens that are sheltered from the rain and wind and use coconut husks to start fires. We have nothing like those facilities. Not far from our house there is a spare open wood barbeque, but once our lighter no longer goes, I have only a magnifying glass to light a fire, so that means cooking during the day. Cooking what?

However, I won't give up, and we won't be here on 11th August. I promise, Shan!

* * *

Andrew invited Juanito to the boat for a boys' movie night a few days ago. Ooo-kaaayyyy. The chief arrived, with another friend in tow, just as I was starting to cook our dinner — back when we actually had food to cook for dinner — so I chucked in another cup of rice, and we all ate together. The idea had been that the kids would go to the house and watch their own movie, but as we got started with the adults' movie, the power went out. Raymond knocked on the door and asked to borrow the battery charger that we had rescued. Once again, the island has power because of our battery charger. By the time everything was sorted out, the kids had to stay with us, and no one watched the movie anyway.

During the course of the evening, Juanito said, with all genuineness, that as this was our home, he didn't mind if I drank alcohol. I thanked him very politely and told him although that was kind, I had had every intention of doing so regardless. To my surprise, he burst out laughing, and said, 'Great answer.' Go figure.

Over the next hour or so, we went over the recipe for yeast and sugar, and the two island men gave me all sorts of advice about proportions and technique, explaining what they were suggesting and why. They quickly finished their tuba, which they shared with me, and then helped polish off our yeast, too. As I was preparing to get more, Juanito called out, 'You're not going to throw that out are you?'

'No, Juanito,' I replied, 'I'm going to get more.' And the world was a happy place.

The night grew older, the kids went to bed, the bottles became emptier and the words started pouring out, as they do. Suddenly, it was a case of, 'Brace yourself, Jenny; here comes what they really think!' But confounding my expectations yet again, Juanito managed to spin me out completely when he thanked Andrew and me for everything we have done.

At that point, I couldn't shut up and blurted out that we had caused nothing but trouble, the islanders don't like us or want us and that we have caused way more hassle than good. I said we felt uncomfortable and that it was clear from the reactions of the islanders that the sooner we are gone the better.

Back came this response: Yes, a certain proportion of the islanders do feel that way about us, and we haven't helped our cause. They will always hate us and that's that. But another proportion of the islanders see things differently. According to Juanito and his friend, the new ideas and new ways of doing things that we have brought in have changed them, hopefully forever. These are their words, not mine.

People see Andrew and I with each other all the time, and now spouses are spending time in public with each other. This was never done before.

They said they have never witnessed such strict discipline enforced on children, and at first the kids hated it, but now they show more respect and have a sense of responsibility for others' possessions. Juanito and his friend have noticed a change in the attitude of children to parents and their authority. There is a 20 per cent higher attendance at school. They are amazed that our girls do as they are told, and other parents are now following our example.

When I read back these words, they sound pretentious, and they're not intended to be. What I am trying to say is the values, methods and priorities that are accepted every day in Australia by Australians, be they kids or adults, are being seen here for the first time.

Apparently the locals want to have a feast in our honour when we leave, and want to give us something to remember them by. As *if* we'd forget! And, hey, we have Moggie Doggie, who has become a beloved feature of island life for all the kids. She is a very happy little lady who is now toilet trained and will sit on command, come when called and bring things, too. Not bad for nine weeks old.

That kind of positive relationship between dogs and humans is yet another thing the Mogmogians have never seen.

A by-product of all this progress with Moggie came out in our interaction with that rude, bossy Jarrod, who has been coming around to our place. At first when he asked if he could come in, I questioned him about why he would want to come into our house of all houses. He shrugged, and asked again. I sighed and agreed. Since then he has come over most days for a while. Once I caught him swearing and yelling when he was mucking around on the Rip Stiks, so I banned him for half an hour. He was as dark as a thunder cloud and yelled at me that his friend had made him say that.

I replied that, no, he had said it; no one had made him say it. 'Don't blame someone else for your own actions,' I said. He stomped off.

An hour later he reappeared, and I said he could play again. He stopped in front of me, apologised for his actions and gave me a bag of rose apples. Wow!

He came again the next day, demanding to know why Colonel, his pup — Moggie's brother — didn't love him the way Moggie loves us. We told him to love the pup and the pup would love him. Back he came a few days later, with a huge grin on his face which was about the size of the grin on his dog. He was playing with Colonel and having a ball. Excitedly, Jarrod called me outside and said, 'Watch this! Colonel, come here!' Colonel raced up to him and leapt into his arms. The look on his face was unforgettable.

Yesterday, Jarrod and I were chatting, and he mentioned Chofung. When I asked him if he missed her, his head went down and he was quiet. After a moment he looked up at me, with tears in his eyes, and just said, 'Yes.'

'I do too,' I said, and he smiled.

TWENTY-EIGHT

WE WITNESS A SPECIAL CELEBRATION

Some days on Mogmog, the sky is so deeply blue that when it melds with the blues of the ocean, it infuses the air with a blueness all of its own. Adding to this is a peculiar stillness, times when you can no longer hear the crashing of waves on the outside of the atoll. Then every sound becomes magnified into the blueness.

It was such a day on Friday, the day of Father Moses's first Mass on Mogmog. Father Moses is a local island boy who was ordained last summer. Although very popular, he ruffled a few feathers when word got around that he wasn't starting his priestly duties on Mogmog. As Juanito is the high chief of all the outer islands, protocol dictates that Father Moses should start his run of first Masses here. However, he would be giving Mass at Falalop and Federai before Mogmog. Juanito calmed the waters by pointing out that Father Moses is not Jesus, he is just a man.

Preparations started five days out from the great day. Palm leaves were picked and left to turn yellow. Locked away from prying eyes, men and women practised dancing at all hours. Working groups were designated jobs, such as cleaning or cooking.

My job was to roast pork for the priest's lunch. That's something you've got to get right. I offered to contribute roast vegies, too, but that had to be changed when no bloody ship turned up to deliver vegies. Two pigs were slaughtered on Wednesday and the pork was delivered to me ceremoniously. My plan was to roast it, using the oven in *Windie*'s galley.

The flower working party outdid themselves. They organised a walkway that stretched all the way from the beach to the church. Banana vine had been sliced into 8-inch pieces that then became vases for floral arrangements that the people wove into the walkway. Two marquees fringed with palm leaves were set up in front of the church, and outside the church was an arch with the word 'Welcome' woven in palm and bougainvillea. There were floats in the water, each with a palm attached to the top, looking as if they'd sprouted in the ocean.

* * *

It was Andrew who came up with the idea of contacting Bill Acker and enlisting his support. An American who lives in Yap, Bill owns the biggest resort and dive operation there.

We had met Bill and had drinks with him at his Manta Bay Resort. The bar at the resort is a large and beautifully restored three-storey trading junk. It has two restaurants, and the cannon is fired every afternoon at 4pm to announce happy hour. A large screen has been installed at the bow, and when weather permits, movies are shown, so patrons can enjoy a pizza, beer and movie. It's wonderful.

Bill, a generous, affable man, and his wife, Patricia, had given us all a warm welcome. They explained that it is a rite of passage to jump into the water from the side of the lugger, and both Barrie girls soon passed through it! Then Patricia wove palm birds for the girls while Bill and Andrew and I chatted.

Back on Mogmog, Andrew's idea was that maybe Bill might know of a boat that could possibly come out to us. Immediately I liked the idea and got onto it. It took a bit of work to get past Bill's minders, but when I did, he was wonderful.

We found Bill's empathy immediately palpable. He had lived on Mogmog in 1976, and quickly tuned in to our situation. I felt like the world had lifted. Yes, he would work something out. He didn't know what, but he wanted our requirements and he would get back to us. The relief!

After that early-morning phone call, Andrew and Diana headed for Falalop. Amos was flying in two boxes of groceries that the store had put together for us. And hopefully there would be mail.

Moses's Mass was scheduled for a few hours later.

Andrew came back with the groceries, which bore little

resemblance to what had been ordered, but hey, we now have food, toilet paper, lighters and frozen vegies.

Gotta love that! And, unexpectedly, two boxes of chocolates!

* * *

As the time of Father Moses's arrival approached, the islanders all gathered to wait for his boat to appear on the horizon. Two traditional outrigger canoes had been positioned in the water as a guard of honour. When Father Moses's boat eventually came into view, everyone started singing and dancing together. Two men stood at the water's edge with huge palm fans, ready to shade Moses as he walked.

The new priest alighted from the boat, dressed in his traditional thu, and was greeted by Ellie and other ladies, who presented leis and floral headdresses. Everyone then followed him as he walked up to the church, singing all the way. It was a welcome worthy of the Pope.

Juanito gave a short welcome speech, to which Moses responded, and then everyone came up singly and in pairs to shake Moses's hand and perhaps bestow more flowers. Juanito introduced Shan, Diana, Andrew and me to Father Moses, and then it was time for the Mass. Because of the length of the Mass, the pork was late getting to the oven. Yikes!

Afterwards, the entire population of Mogmog gathered in the centre of the village. There were so many barbeques going that it was like Perth's Kings Park on Mother's Day. Smoke was everywhere, people were everywhere, and permeating everything were the smells of food: deep-fried fish, donuts, barbequed pork, boiled taro, rice and biscuits (where did *they* come from?). Juanito kept asking about my roast pork. I think he thought I'd forgotten. It came out 20 minutes late but, luckily, perfect. Phew!

Lunch was delicious.

* * *

In the middle of that happy interlude, I slipped back to *Windie* to check my email. Bill Acker had sent me two already.

Bill had agreed to help us expedite the repairs to the supply ship in order to restart the delivery of supplies in the area — and our main aim, of course, was to get the building materials needed to finish off *Windrider*. Our immediate focus was chasing up the missing part for the ship. Earlier, I had tried to phone Dennis in Palau to find out about the part's availability in China. But of course Dennis doesn't work on Fridays. I had tried to get info from someone else, but had drawn a blank there, too. According to Bill's email, he had figured out what the hold-up was:

> The word on the street, and that's normally pretty reliable, is that the part for the ship is ready and waiting in China, but the shipping company don't have enough money to pay for it. How FSM is *that*! They are now in negotiation with the Yap government for funding. It's not going anywhere soon.

Fisheries will do a charter for us out here and bring everything for $3550. Stuff that! We can fly it here for that. Yeah ... Okay ... we can't fly the paints and fuel drums, but you get the idea.

The second of Bill's emails was as follows:

Dear Jenny,

If I understand your list correctly, you have 18 pcs of 2 x 6 x 18, 14 pcs 2 x 4 x 18 and 4 pcs of 2 x 10 x 18?

I think *Popou* [the Manta Bay Resort dive boat] can carry this, unless I am reading your list of lumber wrong. As I said, we would propose, although it's not a deal-breaker, that we put our spare diesel in your avgas drums and then when out there, we empty them into our main tanks so you end up with empty drums. I am assuming that you are using them for floats and not for drinking water? If you need them as clean as possible, we can make other arrangements.

I will help you for cost. We estimate this to be very close to $2000. It will take us roughly 275 gallons of diesel to go roundtrip, and with oil, anti-freeze, staff and a bit for wear and tear, I think $2000 is very close. As I said, I wish we had a better boat in Yap for making runs such as this as *Popou* is designed for diving and speed, not for economical cruising.

I have checked with Fisheries and they are quoting me $3530 to go out there with one of their boats and they say no discounts available. I feel terrible charging $2000, but it's better than what they are saying.

I am also trying to check on the ship and so far have gotten mixed answers. I will keep trying the ship.

This will be the longest email from me as we cannot keep 'em much shorter since we know what we are talking about. One word of caution, if we are bringing any booze, be SURE that it remains hidden or you will be sharing with everyone.

Hang in there,

Bill

Patricia sends her love to the girls. She remembers making them birds.

Gees, you meet some fantastic people. One thing of many I have learned in all of this drama is that your great mates are your great mates, and nothing will ever change that. Sometimes the people you thought were your mates aren't necessarily so. And this is especially hurtful when it's your oldest mates you are talking about. For us there's a host of new mates — the Palauan crowd, Louise in Darwin and now Bill — who make you realise that it doesn't really matter how long you have known someone, the mateship is either there or it isn't. Thanks, Bill.

* * *

Traditional dancing was in full swing when I rejoined the festivities for Father Amos. The women's is slow and graceful and is often performed sitting. The men use sticks and their movements are reminiscent of battles; it's frenetic, exciting and fun. I'd love to see them practise after a few tubas. It'd be hilarious!

After dinner there was more dancing. This time, it was anything but the traditional stuff, and being funny was the order of the day. I realised that the sense of humour of these people is essentially the same as the Aussie sense of humour. For hours, they poked fun at themselves and parodied their traditional dancing. Everyone was in tears of laughter, including us, although we lost a bit in translation.

It was a wonderful night, full of laughter, with the entire village joining in and happy. It was the first time I had seen everyone together having fun.

I went to bed frustratedly optimistic and feeling privileged to have been allowed to be part of a wonderful day.

TWENTY-NINE

THE PETROL SHIP MYSTERY

The day after Father Amos's Mass, Andrew constructed a Moggie ramp on *Windrider*: a long plank extending from the coral up to the back steps of the boat on the starboard side. It took about two minutes for her to be racing up and down and bouncing in and out of the boat as she wishes.

The girls have decided to start sleeping on the boat on the couches. Figures. They trashed bedroom 1, they trashed bedroom 2, so now it's time to start on the boat!

In fact, I've started moving us all back into the boat, bit by bit. It's a big job. Elephants again — you know: one bite at a time. But it's hugely satisfying.

In my treks backwards and forwards from house to boat, I had to return a tub that Raymond had kindly lent us for food ages ago. I stopped to pass the time of day with him and Jolene, and in the course of the conversation, I was able to tell him the sex of his three new kittens. He now has six! No rats over there!

That was when he told me about the funeral boat coming past here on Monday. *What! Stop!* Start again! What's doing what?

'There's a petrol boat coming from Pohnpei, arriving in Yap on Monday, picking up a deceased man and taking him to Laumotrek for burial.'

'Where exactly is the petrol ship going?'

'Leaving Pohnpei today, going to Laumotrek, Fais, Falalop and Yap, and then to Falalop and Laumotrek and Pohnpei. The dead guy worked for Transship, and so they are doing it for him.'

'When you say petrol ship, do you mean it runs on petrol or it delivers petrol?' Naturally, I was thinking about the potential size of the thing and how much timber it could perhaps take.

Raymond shot me a quizzical look. 'No. There are only two petrol ships in the area and they only do 2000 miles.'

None the wiser, I frowned.

'Why don't you ring your embassy and ask?'

Bloody great idea! Minutes later, I phoned the embassy and, being Saturday, no one was there. However, there was an emergency help number. Feeling like a fraud, I called it. The lady who answered was in Canberra and very helpful. I explained what can only have been gobbledigook to her, but she took it in and said she would see if someone named Janet would take my call on a Saturday. Ten minutes later, she rang back and put me through to Janet, who was out having lunch. Janet asked me to email her with all the details and said she would get back to me. I felt like a creep disturbing her.

An hour or so later, I received an email from Janet saying that yes, the info I had from Raymond was essentially correct. It was a patrol ship, and would be getting to Yap no earlier than Wednesday. She is going to see what she can do on Monday to divert the ship from its planned route so it goes past Mogmog for us.

Patrol ship! Duh. There's the petrol ship. What an idiot I had been!

Once I recovered from my embarrassment, I was able to connect the dots. Of course! We had met and become friends with some Australian navy personnel in Palau. Australia has bought a number of naval patrol ships for this region. They are our navy boats and they are supplied with captain and one officer to run and maintain them for the local people. The local people are then employed to work with the Aussies, with a view to eventually taking over the ships. The Aussie crew are navy guys who are deployed here with their families for two-year stints.

Suddenly my palms were sweating and my heart rate shot up! Surely this was going to turn out to be a case of Aussie help Aussie. That's what we do. That's who we are. Aussie mateship is legendary.

* * *

If my plan comes off, it will be a bloody miracle. The patrol ship is due in Yap on Thursday. No word as yet on when it will be leaving. I am doing my utmost to get on Friday's flight out of here and onto that boat.

Amos has set things up so that the rudders, paints and antifouls from Guam, eight empty avgas drums and the inverter are sitting at the dock in Yap. Ali has organised for the timber to be delivered to the same place on the dock. He will then get the food delivered on Friday.

Oh, no! Just heard that the plane is full. Ever since Saturday, when I found out about the patrol ship, I have been trying to ring Tony of PMA to get a seat. It took them until Wednesday to tell me that there is no mobile coverage on Falalop. Thanks, guys! Juanito then took matters into his own hands and sent word to Tony via Eric and Tim, two Norwegian tourists who were passing through, that I was to be on that plane no matter what. Someone would have to be bumped. I felt bad and was trying to work out how else we could coordinate this, but Andrew and Juanito were adamant that this was the only way it could all work.

Friday dawned, and in the absence of other choices, we decided to take the dinghy to Falalop. That way, I could make it back quickly and get on the phone if I couldn't get on the flight. The embassy had emailed to say the ship was dockside in Yap.

Andrew and I left early and got to the airport first. When Tony arrived, he stated that the plane was full, and that was that. We pleaded our case, but he was far from impressed. Then Amos landed and, by a stroke of luck, a party of four had become a party of three, so I was on.

Now get this. PMA is a 'missionary' service. Over the preceding four weeks, people had been bumped four times, and here they were getting bumped again. Who should get off the plane but one of the big cheeses of PMA and his daughter and son-in-law! There for a pleasure jaunt, they then proceeded to tour the island while we all waited for them ... and waited ... and waited. It was incredibly rude. Over an hour later, this fellow toddled back to the plane so we were able to let him know that Amos was off looking for him. Unbelievable.

Eventually, I waved goodbye to Andrew as we taxied down the runway. We turned and flew low over Mogmog, so I got to wave at the kids, too. In fact Amos flew quite low full-stop, way more than he usually does. Of course the grand fromage was on board, wasn't he?

After a perfect touchdown in Yap, I bummed a ride into town with Eric and Tim. Having made it this far, my first priority was to get to the bank. Grabbing a Smirnoff Ice on the way, I raced over there. Heavens, I was on a roll!

Took out my newly validated card and inserted it into the ATM. The words 'Invalid card' flashed across the screen. *No!* Tried again: 'Invalid card'. Oh, shit! Tried Andrew's card. 'Insufficient funds'. Oh, shit again. That's the trouble with having no damned internet banking: you have no way of fixing this sort of problem yourself, as you would do in Australia without blinking. So now I had no money! Frankly, I had bigger fish to fry. Off to the dock I dashed: I had a boat to meet, load, catch — no time to waste worrying about petty details like payment.

With difficulty, I made my way to the patrol boat, which had parked on the wrong side of the wharf. Not the most convenient spot! Then, in the blink of an eye, I changed from being stressed to chuffed as a chorus of 'Jenny!' went out, and it was like a Mogmog party on the dock. Laurie, the teacher, was working on the boat, and he had all our lumber stacked and on board. The hold was groaning with our food supplies, including 1200 pounds of staples Andrew and I were donating to the locals. That sorted, Laurie was busying himself with the rudders and avgas drums. I let out a huge sigh of relief. Against the odds, I might just be able to pull this off. Fantastic!

Now it was time to meet Jim, the captain. It turned out that he had had a blinder in Yap the night before, and he was nowhere to be seen. Instead I found someone called Simeon, and he took me through the hold and showed me the inverter and the antifouls. Phew. So now we had everything on board, but I wasn't sure what food had been packed.

Andrew phoned to see how things were going, so I asked him to transfer funds to another account. Believe me, that was no small request: Andrew loathes anything to do with banks. He won't even use an ATM unless it's totally unavoidable. Never before had I asked him to do phone banking, so he was a bundle of nerves. Funny, isn't it? This is a guy who can singlehandedly rebuild a boat; just don't get him anywhere near a bank.

To my relief, he rang back triumphantly. Eureka! He had done it! I asked him to try to sort out the invalid card, even though it was mine and I didn't hold out much hope there.

A woman on a mission, I sped back to the bank and withdrew the daily limit. My next destination was the store — to get the invoices, so I would know what we had been given. Finally, I met Ali in person, which was fantastic. As he hadn't packed the freezer goods, he didn't have the invoices ready. Could I come back at three? Okay.

On I raced to Amos's house to pay him for the ticket. I still owed him $700, which I had hoped to pay then and there. Unfortunately, Andrew had had no luck with activating my card. Every so often a card is a dud, and that must have been the case here. How bloody frustrating!

But there was no time to dwell on that as I still had two hardware places to call in on, and they were at either end of town. By now, I was exhausted and running on empty. I hadn't eaten yet that day.

With that sorted, it was back to the store to get the invoices, and then I retraced my footsteps to the boat to ask what time I should be on board. The answer was 5.30 for 6pm. That was fine. Better than fine, because then I was free. I had nothing left to do.

I decided to walk up to the Manta Ray Resort for a glass of wine. Bill Acker was in the pool. I was glad to be able to thank him in person; he's a terrific guy! Eric and Tim met me at the bar so I got to sit with friends over a drink, laughing and joking. It was such a treat to do that after all these months. Nevertheless, I kept a close eye on the clock, as I still had to finalise things with Ali.

With time to spare, I met Ali at the shop, and he told me he had just gone to take the frozen stuff onto the boat, and it had left already. At first the seriousness of the situation didn't hit me; he had to be joking. But he wasn't! I sprinted down to the wharf, from where I could see the boat on the horizon, and it was barely 5.30. Honestly, I could not believe my eyes.

Andrew rang at that exact moment, and he was pretty pissed off at me for missing the thing. But, hey, I was on time! The boat had to have left at 5pm to get to where they were.

Suddenly Aiden, Juanito's son, arrived from nowhere. I flew up to him and received a huge hug. Wasting no time, I immediately filled him in on my predicament. With an air of urgency, he grabbed his phone, only to slap his forehead in exasperation as he realised it was out of credit. Hang on a sec; I had Juanito's in my pocket. I handed it to Aiden, and he vanished. Within minutes, he came flying up in a ute, yelling at me to get in.

By then, Tim and Eric were yelling, a heap of islanders were yelling, Aiden was yelling; it was madness. I leapt into the back of the ute, and Aiden told me that the patrol boat's dinghy was coming back for me. Crikey!

Could Aiden and I make it to the store for the frozen stuff, I asked. More yelling that there wasn't time. I was convinced that there was time … and Aiden decided to give it a go.

Ali had kept the shop open for me, and as soon as they caught sight of us, the guys in the shop started yelling and carting stuff out to the ute.

Then Aiden and I were back in the ute, heading for the wharf. Waved at Eric and Tim as we drove past. Dead-heated it with the dinghy. More yelling as the dinghy was loaded, and then I was in.

Waved to Aiden and Laurie, and flung $40 at Laurie for beer for the guys, and then we were pulling out from the wharf. Unbelievable.

Meanwhile, unknown to me, Andrew had got hold of Bill Acker and lined up a chase boat if I needed it. Wow! What a team!

Now I was on my way home to Mogmog, and Andrew had no idea if I was on the boat or not. And we were out of mobile range.

Safely aboard the patrol boat, I perched on the stern on the timber and calmed myself down. After chatting to some crew I discovered the patrol boat was from Fremantle, our home port. Turns out the crew had been trained at Garden Island, just off the WA coast. We had so many similar memories; the boat was like a slice of home.

Then I was shown to my cabin ... What! A cabin? I'd expected to sit on a pile of wood for the night. Rita, a Peace Corps worker, answered the knock on the door and let me in. It was a two-bunk cabin, and she had chosen the top bunk.

I had brought wine, so we had a wine each and chatted. Rita was keen to get settled as it was going to be a rough trip. Just before she took her Dramamine and excused herself, she showed me our bathroom. Wow again! A clean toilet and shower just for Rita and me. This was an incredible bonus.

Somehow, I'd got the feeling from the crew that the cabin was where I should stay, so that's what I made up my mind to do. It meant skipping dinner, but I was getting used to that. When I'd weighed in at the airport, I'd been 100 lbs, or just over 45 kilograms, and that included my bag. Normally I weigh 62–65 kilograms, so this is a big change for me.

Sleep struck me as a good idea, so I put my head down. I don't know how much later on it was when I was woken by a Micronesian who insisted I was in his normal bed and he would have to share with me. I said he could lie top to toe, and that was that. Over the next hours he kept groping at me as I tried to sleep. Eventually, disgusted, I gave up on the idea of sleep and went up onto the bridge. I guess you can't have it all.

It was about 5am when I was greeted on deck by the now familiar figure of Simeon. 'Of course,' he said when I asked if I could use the VHF.

'Sailing vessel *Windrider*. Sailing vessel *Windrider*. Sailing vessel *Windrider*. This is FSS *Independence*. FSS *Independence*. FSS *Independence*. Do you read? Over.'

Silence.

'Sailing vessel *Windrider*. Sailing vessel *Windrider*. Sailing vessel *Windrider*. This is FSS *Independence*. FSS *Independence*. FSS *Independence*. Do you read? Over.'

Then, 'Heavens! I read you loud and clear, *Independence*. How are you, Jen?'

You know how you respond to the voice of your loved ones. To hear Andrew almost made me cry. 'I'm fine and we have an ETA at Mogmog in 50 minutes. Request dinghy and help.'

'We have dinghies and men waiting as we speak. We will meet you in 50 minutes.'

'I love you!'

'I love you too!' [Not your standard VHF speak!]

* * *

It was a blustery 6am when we arrived to see six boats and 60 men all waiting to help. Andrew burst off the first boat and flew up to hug me. The grin on his face was so heartwarming.

I spotted my creepy, gropey night visitor, so I took him over and introduced him to my husband. 'Andrew, this is the guy that groped my tits all night. Gropey guy, this is my husband, Andrew.'

The atmosphere was euphoric. As I landed on the island, Juanito made his way down and welcomed me with a huge grin, and an even huger hug. I was so happy to be able to tell him what Aiden had done to rescue me. Juanito was so pleased.

Unknown to me, the shop on Mogmog was expecting a consignment of stores from the petrol boat. So the local guys ended up working for hours offloading all our stuff, as well as food for the islanders. As far as I was concerned that was fair enough; there would have been no fresh stores, had it not been for the Australian Embassy in Pohnpei.

Everyone on Mogmog, including us, was back in business.

THIRTY

AGAINST ALL MOGS

A wound on my finger has just managed to explode by itself. All of us have had lots of these infected cuts, but this is a ripper. Even though I started antibiotics in the middle of the night, I feel thoroughly unwell. The swelling goes halfway up my arm. This morning, Andrew had to cut off my wedding ring as I was losing circulation.

Last Sunday, in church, Juanito made mention of how we got the patrol boat to drop supplies here. I didn't understand all he said, but afterwards a number of people came up apologising for stealing our stuff. We made light of it, but crumbs, what a rollercoaster.

Later in the day, I visited Ludis, a lovely older lady who brings us limes all the time. She'd asked if she could buy coffee from us and was clear that she wanted to pay us for it. When I turned up with the coffee and a box of choccies, Ludis had no money on her and wasn't going to accept the coffee. I told her how expensive limes are in Yap, and how much we appreciate the ones she gives us. She cried and said I was her friend in God always. I really like Ludis.

Next morning, there was a bag of limes on the step.

Andrew and I have been working so hard on the boat this week. The glassing is all but finished, and Andrew has started faring today. Faring is when you use a powder and resin mix to smooth off the bottom of the boat. Antifouling will be next.

Through the week, the girls and I have moved most of our stuff out of the house, so we are now living permanently on the boat. It's so wonderful to be home again. We still have to trek up to use the loo, but you can't have everything.

While we were sort of half in the house and half in the boat, I went back to the bathroom to find that all our toiletries had been nicked. Three shampoos, two conditioners and three antiperspirants had 'gone west'. Not a hugie, but it was … you know. We had given and given and given, and when we stopped giving, the Mogs stole. Consequently, now we stink.

Andrew saw red. He grabbed a bag and stomped over the island retrieving our DVDs, which we'd loaned to various people. After he'd got most of them back, he stomped off to Juanito and vented. Juanito was upset and promised to try and get back our toiletries.

Raymond found two empty shampoo containers near the house. At least I felt vindicated in making the accusation. Juanito came up later with soap for us; I politely declined his offer as we had lost no soap. He asked to use the phone and rang Aiden to ask him to buy us more and bring it with him when he comes to Mogmog, which will be soon.

* * *

It's several days since I last wrote. We estimate that we have two weeksish of work to do to finish the boat.

A course of antibiotics later, my finger is still a mess, but at least it is bleeding now, so there's blood flow.

A pup bit Andrew on the toe yesterday, and now that is badly swollen. He woke last night with the nodes in his groin swollen. Shit! Not good. This morning he is very unwell, so more antibiotics for him. Are we going to make it through this last fortnight? Chook has a cold, and Shan's lethargic, which is very out of character.

The emails from Palau are coming thick and fast, bringing weather reports and updates of who's doing what. It seems that Jay and Virian are heading back to Palau from the Philippines, and Danny and Yvonne are on their way back from New Zealand, complete with Vegemite and Cadburys for us. Can't wait to see them, especially Jay. His weather watch over us has been invaluable, and every email ends, 'Hugs, J.' It is impossible to convey the value of these messages, especially as we get closer to leaving. Thanks, guys!

This boat has become our haven; we hide here. We need to have a small place that's sacrosanct. Last Friday, just as we had shut the door, switched on the air-con and turned on the TV, Juanito showed up. Andrew was in the shower when he spotted Juanito walking down the beach in our direction. This sent all us girls diving for shorts or pants to wear, as this has become a pants-free zone once the door is shut.

We have mended a lot of bridges with Juanito. My feelings for him now remind me of the sometimes exasperating relationship most of us have with our parents. I am fond of him, no two ways about it, but I need my space, too. When he made it to the top of the ladder, it was immediately apparent that he had had a fair whack of tuba. Pretty much the first thing he said to us was that he was out of tuba and could he have a beer?

This was too much for Andrew. He has become angrier and angrier throughout the past week. At times he snaps, and it's like living with his father. We decided the quickest way to be alone was to feed Juanito and speed the visit through. Sure enough, 10 tons of food and six beers later, and carrying a packed-up dinner for his grandson, he was on his way.

Andrew was furious, and didn't snap out of it. Apparently he copped an off bit of carrot in his dinner; mine was fine. That was the end of any chance of restoring our peaceful evening.

By then I had had enough of the day and stomped off to bed, where I lay and stewed and stewed and stewed. This lot were not going to undo us as a family; we're stronger than that. I was not going to let Andrew get under my skin and I was not going to let him descend from where he already was. He was becoming so bitter and angry. It was like being around an angry broom.

Andrew slept on the couch — and developed diarrhoea. Perfect. The next two days he had stomach cramps and the runs, and we had no toilet on *Windrider*. Fantastic. He stayed on the couch.

I refuse to let it get to me. Again, we have bigger fish to fry.

* * *

A funeral was held on Friday for a guy who grew up here. It was a huge event. People were arriving for days in the lead-up. Two fishing boats were due from Yap, one of them bringing Aiden, I heard.

Andrew was invited for men's drinks after the funeral. Diana, Shannon and I had a girls' night in and had lots of laughs. It was great.

At midnight, Andrew reappeared at the boat and said I was to go down to the men's house.

To the men's house?

Juanito had invited me. There were men unloading the two fishing boats that had just come in from Yap. Party time!

So I went. And sure enough it was a blast looking at all the food that was coming to the island. A man I hadn't seen before told me to leave. Quietly, I told him I had been invited.

'Leave.'

'The chief invited me.'

'Leave now!'

My blood was boiling; my feelings of delight of a few seconds ago replaced by fury in the blink of an eye.

As I picked my way through the throng, the priest, Father Nick, told me I needed to have more respect and know my place as a woman. And that from the spiritual leader!

I was well clear of the gathering when Andrew caught up with me. Although at first I said there was no way I was staying where I was not welcome, I did turn back. I marched straight up to Juanito. He needed to know what was going on. The chief kept grabbing my hand and telling me to stay. I told him absolutely no way.

My blood boils when I think about the hypocrisy on this island. How can anyone accept and take on one hand, and then reject the giver in the next breath?

With Andrew following close behind, I stormed home. I ranted at him, but what could he do? After a while, he went back to the party. Apparently Juanito wanted to come and see me. Andrew suggested that another time might be a better idea. The chief has kept clear of me since that incident.

Yet again I had fucked up, with no intention of doing so. Yet again I had been excited and happy for these people, only to have them tear that down.

* * *

Kevin, a nice guy, came to visit yesterday and had a few beers with us. The subject of the funeral party came up and he told it to me as it is. I am very grateful to him for that.

Here's the go: women are loved and respected but they are a second-class group — behind men in every way. As a woman, I should be spending my day with the other women. That is my place. Because I spend my day with my husband, I am not liked by the women.

I act more in the stereotypical role of a man on Mogmog, so the men hate me because I do not have the correct respect for their superiority, as demonstrated by my not spending the days with the women.

Bottom line is that Andrew is liked and admired by the men. I am not liked by anyone.

Finally, everything is stripped bare. It's a relief really. The hypocrisy is at an end. The Mogmog people don't like me. Fine. I need no friends here. But that's also the end of the giving. They take and take and take, and if they can't take they steal. They'll let me get them food, and ships, and then they steal the betel nut bags that I had bought just as a gesture — 11 bags disappeared from my house.

Two weeks to go. Against all Mogs.

THIRTY-ONE

TRUE BLUE

I sit here now listening to John Williamson. Of our six remaining CDs — the rest have been stolen — two are John's. I would love to meet him. He has given definition to us as Aussies, telling us through his music that 'we can do this' in spite of the difficulties. He has reminded us to look at the good and to be proud. He emphasises the important things in life, like valuing each other, family, love, having fun and the Aussie way. Thank you, John.

Also among our six is a Roy Orbison compilation. That one we do not play. 'Pretty Woman' has become our boat's signature tune. Every time we pull up anchor on our way to a new destination, we crank out 'Pretty Woman' to as many decibels as we can take. That CD stays away until it's time to play 'Pretty Woman' again.

We'll be hearing that song soon. Today we hoisted the

starboard engine into the boat. Just the two of us did that. It fits. It's in. Later today we fire her up. The starboard hull is ready for epoxy primer and antifoul. The starboard rudder is in.

It looked like we were going to be short of resin, so I racked my brains and thought of this great guy in Guam who we've purchased from. I flicked off an email asking if he knew of anyone who might have what we need. Instantly the reply came back with a name, email address and phone number. Later that day the resin was on a plane to Yap. Moments like that give you goose bumps.

* * *

There were two buckets. Each had a crab in the bottom. One crab was Yapese, the other was from Guam. The crab from Guam was sitting there feeling sorry for himself when another crab, who happened to be from Guam also, came by. The crab walking by asked why he was in the bucket. He explained he had fallen in, so the crab from Guam reached in and helped the other crab out of the bucket.

Another Yapese crab was walking past the Yapese crab in the bucket and stopped and asked what he was doing there. The crab in the bucket reached up and grabbed the walking crab and pulled him down into the bucket. Then he waited for the next crab to come by. Eventually, he had enough crabs in the bucket that he could climb over them all, stand on their heads and walk off the top of them out of the bucket.

Juanito told us that, ages ago. I haven't laid eyes on him for a long time now.

* * *

Someone unscrewed the radiator caps on our newly repaired engines. We never did find those caps. Then they carefully poured sand into the cooling system, leaving no trace of sand in the thread. There was no sand near the engines, so they went to the trouble to bring it up from the beach. Clearly, the saboteur was an adult who knows what they are doing.

What is with these people? They don't want us here, so why slow us down! Our anger was difficult to contain.

When the going gets tough, the tough get going! We closed ranks, got in the boat, shut the door and — determined not to be beaten — sent yet another email to Jeff Frazer from Yanmar. As well as requesting technical advice re the sand, we asked if there were caps in Australia that we could get yesterday. An immediate reply from Jeff had the caps being overnighted out of Melbourne within the next few hours, and contained promising tech advice: all might be okay.

Yet again, we are reminded of what it means to be Australian! From the bottom of our hearts, thanks so much, Jeff! We thought we'd be here for another six weeks waiting on mail, but we should have the new radiator caps in about a week. We decided to keep that news under our hats.

* * *

Since the night of the funeral party, I have been keeping my mouth shut and staying out of everyone's way. In the last week, I have gone nowhere and have spoken only when I've been spoken to — not in a shitty way, just in a 'keeping out of your way' kind of way. It seems to be the right thing to do.

We emailed Janet at the embassy to keep her informed of what has been happening, and her quite strong advice was that we may need to get out of here without the boat. I see her point of view but I hope we can avoid that.

This week we have been crook as dogs. The girls have some kind of lurgy and Andrew and I have diarrhoea very badly; I spent two days in bed with waves of terrible stomach pains. The loo is just too far away, so the ocean it is.

The grossness of it all brings to mind having kids. I remember going into St John's to have Diana, and a lovely midwife cheerfully asked me if I had left my dignity at the front door. When I looked quizzical, she stated with a smile that I could pick it up on my way out.

* * *

Juanito, Juanito, Juanito. He and I are never on firm footing for long. I have seen him only briefly since last Friday, now a week ago. Andrew has had a couple of drinks with him.

Last night Andrew went to the men's house. He tottered home at about 1.30, feeling very different about things. The men there claimed no knowledge of any of the thefts, and proclaimed undying assistance to the end to help us off Mogmog. Even Falalai, Chofung's owner, was chiming in.

Pardon my scepticism. Here's my view: Andrew is now acting as a man in a man's world, and his woman is where she is supposed to be: tucked up at home. Fine. See if I care. My fish will be fried in about 10 days, when we take off outta here and leave all those Mogmog men behind.

One of the guys came home with Andrew in the wee tiny hours to have a drink with me. That seemed like a nice gesture. I got dressed and went down to where we have a camp set up under the boat. After we'd been chatting and drinking for a while, he felt compelled to explain men's superiority. Even though I assured him it was unnecessary, he insisted.

And guess what? According to our guest, men are superior because they can hold their breath. Yep, that's it! Evidently women can do everything else, but they can't hold their breath to spear a fish, and women don't understand how hard it is to bottomfish for two whole hours for dinner.

Right! Silly me! I'll just tuck my Padi Dive Master card back in my wallet, deflate the dinghy and be off to the taro patch then!

* * *

Moggie Doggie has become the happy sunlight in our days. She is the queen of all she surveys, courtesy of the 'Moggie Doggie loggie', the plank that goes from the ground up to the back deck. She tears up and down the ramp and flies up and down the steps and over the top deck. Every morning she races up to the top deck, goes to our hatch and jumps on it if it's shut; if it's open, she jumps through it. See, drop bears really *do* exist! A fluffy barrel with a cheeky smile, Moggie has made her place firmly in the centre of our collective family heart.

The other day, when things were really bad — with Andrew and I doubled up in pain, and the kids down for the count with the 'flu — we started a tally of the number of times she made us happy, smile or laugh. As a family we gave up after we got to 20 in less than an hour. We love you, Moggie.

As I finish off this chapter, I'm still listening to John Williamson's 'Boomerang Café' and thinking of Andrew and me and our own Boomerang Café. It was part of our lives when we first met in 1977, when we were 12, at the band hall downstairs in the Young Australia League building — the YAL — in Murray Street, Perth. And that's where we met every Monday night until well after we married.

Thanks for reminding me of what really counts, John.

THIRTY-TWO

ANNIVERSARIES

This Saturday is the annual general meeting of the Mogmog Tuba Drinkers' Association. Yes, really. The function of the association is to determine who can drink tuba.

On Mogmog there is no defined drinking age. Rather, each case is assessed on its merits. Consequently, the drinking age can be anywhere from 17 to 25. The association specifies which trees a drinker may use to manufacture tuba, and how many he can have operational at any time. The vice-president and secretary are designated as the panel to determine tuba-related punishments, usually suspension of drinking rights.

Let me introduce you to this year's office-bearers. The president is Kevin. Currently he is nursing three broken ribs and has his hand bandaged. Last week, he fell out of his tuba tree in the middle of the night, pissed. The vice-president is Glen, the guy who had his hand crushed by our boat. Glen subsequently admitted that he had been drinking since dawn that day. The secretary is Falalai, last owner of Chofung and father to Jarrod. This means that it falls to Glen and Falalai to determine who can and who cannot drink. There's a certain irony in that, methinks.

Raymond and Mike have both just completed their three-month suspension after the night of the torch-smashing and coral-dragging. They have largely abided by the restrictions. We bought them a bottle of Bacardi each when the boat last came. Last Sunday, Raymond's birthday, they made an appeal to the panel, but the panel decided not to allow them to drink. Again, the hypocrisy of the place! However, the pair are allowed to drink on Saturday at the AGM. But only for the AGM.

The AGM is the day of the year when all the men in the Tuba Drinkers' Association get together for the elections and then proceed to drink — all day and all night.

Now no one can call me a prude, but I really don't think these guys need a designated and organised drinking day. They drink all day and all night at the best of times. It's safe to say that if they're awake, they're drinking. Juanito's greatest aim with tuba drinking is to try to convince the men to wait until lunchtime, so that at least part of the day can be productive.

On a more serious note, I am actually a bit concerned about Saturday. We have decided that Andrew should go along and be with the men, to try to diffuse anything that may occur when a whole heap of drunken men come up with a great idea.

I am staying in the boat with the girls, with the door locked. We have two cattle prods on board, and while I don't anticipate using them, that option will be on hand, if necessary, and will do no lasting harm.

* * *

Lately, the weather has been shocking and is slowing us down. Andrew has all but finished sanding the starboard hull. Yesterday was spent trying to locate a part from Yanmar that had been sent six weeks ago. We found that it was sent to Palau by a well-meaning freight-forwarder, and is currently MIA. After much stress, we located a secondhand one in Perth.

Then it was a question of organising to freight it here. To our horror, the logistics company DHL wanted $250 for 2 kilograms! Luckily, after we rang friends with an account, that was all sorted.

That's not the full extent of our problems. Continental Airlines has been refusing to transport the hardener for the epoxy resin we need to finish the port hull on the grounds that it's a safety hazard. Strangely, the fact that they flew four times the amount of the exact same product last month has been overlooked. I had given up on getting the stuff from Guam and was preparing to go through Brisbane. The arrangements were almost finalised when I received an email from Guam saying Continental Airlines would transport it after all. I'll believe that when I see it. It is stressful to be so close to having a seaworthy boat and yet to be thwarted constantly. It adds greatly to the general level of anxiety.

As we get closer and closer to achieving our goal, the smallest deviation from what we're expecting has an inordinately significant impact on morale and demeanour. Yesterday, I tried to scare Andrew as a joke and he reacted really badly. He's wound up so tight that when he sits down to eat, he remains silent, and does nothing but slowly and deliberately shovel forkfuls of food into his mouth. He walks deliberately, he works deliberately, he even sleeps deliberately. Every step is a step towards leaving, every movement calculated towards one end. It's awful to watch.

When I say we're nearly there, he withdraws like a snail going into a shell, as he feels there is too much that is beyond our control and that setting timeframes is useless. Once the part and the resins arrive, there will be nothing further that will be needed and very little left to do.

However, this morning we woke to lightning and driving rain, which means there will be no sanding or painting of hulls today. A sense of pervading vagueness and an unsettling lack of direction fall over the day. It's another day here unnecessarily.

To fill in time usefully, Andrew started to repair Juanito's outrigger canoe. Another side project — Juanito is not aware what Andrew is doing — it has holes that need to be fibreglassed, and it sinks. When it is finished, it will have a foam floor so that it can't sink. This will be glassed in place, all the holes patched, and the outrigger reinforced with glass. Once finished, the island will have all three traditional boats up and running.

As I write, today is Wednesday. It's Andrew's birthday on Friday. He's never been good at birthdays and wants to let it slide with no mention. To Andrew, birthday, are just markers; he determines the success of his life by looking at the achievements of each passing year. As his father died at 53, a part of him figures he's on the home stretch himself. But I have plans for Andrew that will keep him busy till he's at least 100. There's no way he's going the same way as his father.

Our plan to be in Palau for his birthday will not eventuate. With luck, we will make it for Shan's on the 11th. Andrew and Shan have decided that they will share a birthday this year, on Shan's day. We will bust our guts to be in Palau by that date and then we will organise a joint party for the two of them.

Shan is a generous little soul, and is absolutely delighted to share her birthday with 'my gorgeous daddy'.

* * *

The frustrations just keep on coming. At what point do you break? At what point would it be acceptable to break? At what point would someone reading this stop saying, 'Toughen up, Princess'? I have no way of knowing. But today, and it's only 9.30am, the island has been put on rations for diesel because there's not going to be a ship coming to bring more in the near future. This means that the power plant is now going to be turned off between 8am and 6pm.

To solve this, Andrew is wanting to run the installed engine for power. But that needs some serious cooling. Late yesterday he ran a hose into the ocean to use sea water for cooling, but then he started to fear the pump had given up the ghost. Fortunately, this turned out not to be the case, but we desperately need gravity water feed, or a pump for cooling. Miraculously, he found an old pump. It has now seized.

The alternative is for me to spend the day like the sorcerer's apprentice, getting ocean water and filling a huge tub that the engine sits in.

Round we go again on the same old merry-go-round: we're running low on food. The plane due on Friday is full, so we can't get food until Monday. We'll cope.

To help bridge the gap, I decided to make some biscuits. Even though it meant using valuable ingredients, I thought it might be a pick-me-up. We ran out of gas just when I tried to light the oven. That's a bummer, as not only could I not bake my biccies, it means no more warm showers. And no more oven.

As the biscuit mix sits lonely on the bench, I have dug out the single gas burner, the one that runs on butane cans. We have 16 butane cans. Should be okay.

Now it's raining, so Andrew can't sand the hulls anyway. Solves the pump problem for the moment.

Still, I find myself thinking, 'How much can a koala bear?'

* * *

Andrew's birthday was surprisingly fun. He woke with no idea that it was his day. A good start … no, really! Then Sarah, who had asked us when we first arrived when our respective birthdays were, came up wishing him a happy day. Turns out she had spread the word. He ended up with five beautiful leis.

Then Juanito came by with a cake he had made, and Juanito bakes a mean cake. His son does it professionally in Hawaii. Then Raymond came up with a platter that would look right at home in Doyles, the high-class seafood restaurant in Sydney. He had boiled coconut crabs then defleshed them; mixed the flesh with lime, coconut, pepper and so on; and then put the mix back to present them in individual shells. It was sensational. We took the day a bit easy and drank too much, so a fantastic day all round.

Saturday rolled around, and with it the Tuba Drinkers' Association annual meeting. It was a peaceful, happy day, and all suspended drinkers were given the nod to partake once more.

Seriously, the island has a happier feel to it now. Maybe it's because we're nearly there with *Windie*.

THIRTY-THREE

CRUNCH TIME

Monday dawned, and with it the realisation that this was probably our last week on Mogmog. Andrew gets so antsy when I say things like that, but even he admitted over coffee that we now had to say 'when' rather than 'if', and that the 'when' is almost imminent.

First things first: were we going to receive food supplies? I rang Ali, who was late for work. At the airport sorting out our order perhaps? My faith in Ali has grown tremendously over the months. He is a good man. Andrew scoffed.

Then I phoned Amos to check whether our resins and sanding disks had made it on board the plane. Again, a scoff came from behind me. Yet my optimism was well placed: Amos had all our gear stowed, including two big boxes from Ali. Bless his cotton socks!

I rang Ali to express my gratitude for his service, and in return I received an official company thank you for dealing with them over the months. This will, I think, be our final transaction with the Yap general store. They have let me run the account over $4000, way more than at first, and I could just run off into the blue.

We are in debt to Amos, too, to the tune of about $1000, without there being a murmur from him. Sorting out that bill is job number two after we get to Palau. Job number one is sitting down at Sam's bar with a burger, fries and a huge glass — as in glass glass, not plakky glass — of wine with ice. My whole demeanour has changed.

Suddenly there is real light at the end of the tunnel, and as I picture the scene in Palau, a spontaneous grin creeps over my face.

The week crawls on, and suddenly it's Tuesday. Andrew is back from picking up the supplies, which were dropped off in Falalop, and he has all the stuff we asked for except two bags of spuds.

Oh, well, you can't have everything.

To my surprise, he has brought back every last one of the belongings I had left in storage with Ali, who'd kept all of it perfectly safe and had it boxed up and intact for me. I hadn't expected that; this is Micronesia.

All the materials for the boat that Tim sent from Guam seem perfect. Right now, Andrew is making the frame and will have it finished today. We started the epoxy undercoat yesterday, and gees it's gluggy. The rollers are falling to bits after about 10 minutes, but we are assured that brushes will work. It's very slow drying though, which is a pest.

Only two small problems are on our minds at the moment, which means the picture is way brighter than normal. The weather is the first of them. It rains and rains and rains, and while it rains, we can't paint. The other thing is that Mogmog is now completely out of diesel. This means no power. This means no refrigeration, TV, lighting … nothing. At least no one wants our DVDs any more! On top of that, there's no more gas on the island either, so no more fishing in the non-traditional sense. That makes it very difficult, particularly for the elderly, when there's no refrigeration.

Andrew and I have the only diesel on the island. If the islanders' need is greater than ours, we could be in trouble. We got up early and have brought our precious supply down to the boat. We also have the only freezer, and in the past, both Raymond and Juanito have been very generous to us with their freezer space. Heaven knows how we'll juggle that one.

So we'll hide down here with our TV and lights and freezer and hope for the best.

When is this situation likely to be rectified? No one knows. It really says something when a power company is willing to take money in advance for a service it knows it cannot provide — and has no way of providing in the foreseeable future. The awful thing is that it is taking money from people who barely have the means to pay.

* * *

'Making love to you is like making love to a broom.'

'Yeah? Well, making love to you is like making love to a pick-up stick. If I don't hang onto you, you'll fall off the pile!'

With an attack of the giggles, we realised we had discovered a possible cure for a midlife crisis. Just lose 40ish kilos between you, and it feels like being a teenager again — all awkward bony bits everywhere. Try it!

* * *

Another week has gone by. The island is still on diesel rations, but the supply ship is at Falalop. Broken down again, naturally. At least it has offloaded diesel there, so as long as we — the island — can come up with enough outboard fuel between us, we can access the diesel we need.

Andrew and I started applying the two-part epoxy undercoat. Turns out, it's as thick as clay. Andrew was furious. All his hard work was going to be covered in a coat of goob that looks like shit and will take a couple of knots off our speed. He ranted and raved and tried to talk me into leaving for Palau with the girls, saying he would order from Brisbane the stuff he had wanted in the first place and join us in a month. Fat bloody chance!

We chucked it on as thinly as possible, and it was still wet three days later. Being a two-part epoxy, its drying is a chemical reaction and should therefore be quick and definite. After three days had passed, Andrew was furiously sweating about it and started sanding the goob off the hulls. I should say 'trying to sand', as the goob was glugging the sanding belts and binding them to the sander. Not a good few days. So close, we were, and then that.

After time and space and thought and a drink or three, we concluded we would have to do the best we could with what we have.

'I'm going to take it out of the water and do it properly the first opportunity I get.'

My mouth stayed firmly shut. 'Not if it's going to further impinge on this trip, you're not,' methinks.

The paint is also making the rollers fall apart. We can't get any more. Again, let's do the best we can with what we have.

Finally, the starboard hull is complete in every way … by Shan's 10th birthday. So much for swearing that come hell or high water we wouldn't be on Mogmog for her birthday! I felt so bad for her, and found the situation really, really difficult to come to terms with.

First thing in the morning, I went in to greet her in bed, and she sat up brightly and gave me a huge hug, then headed into her birthday with not a single present. For her special-request brekkie, I made pancakes. Everyone who knows me knows that's a very bad idea. I firmly believe there are some things that certain individuals will simply never master, so are best to forget about and move on. For me, pancakes is one of those things. But that's what the birthday girl wanted so that's what she got. And, amazingly, for the first time ever, they worked!

As the day progressed, three ladies came by with beautiful leis for Shan, and eventually her grin took over her whole face. After lunch she made her only request for the afternoon. Could we play games together? Out came Connect 4, Rumble in the Jungle and Jenga, and we spent a fun couple of hours together.

After chicken and rice for dinner, Shannon wanted to make an announcement: 'I would just like to say that I have had a wonderful birthday, and you have made me feel so special. Thank you for making me so happy.'

After she had gone to bed with a kiss and a smile, I sat there and wondered how the hell we ended up with such a great kid. Two years running we have been stuck somewhere repairing the boat on her special day. When eventually we get to Palau, we are going to give this girl the best birthday ever.

* * *

The ship bringing the diesel duly arrived. Ahead of time, I had tried to get some food supplies loaded onto the boat and was told in no uncertain terms that it was a Power Company charter for diesel only: no goods, no passengers. But not to stress, as the ship was going straight back to Yap and would return to Mogmog within days. Hmmmm. As I watched all the people pouring off the ship, with food and goods flying everywhere, and the line of stevedoring men moving the sacks of rice up to the store, I had a feeling things weren't going to go my way. I tried to contact the ship via VHF but they wouldn't respond. Then I rang them, and was told that there is no need for another ship now, so the next one will be here at the end of the month.

Once again, we are ridiculously low on food. We have no fruit or veg of any kind. Andrew and I are skipping breakfast. I'm halving the meat in the meals. After we'd got down to noodles, two cans of sardines and three cans of corned beef, I went to the store and managed to buy a 50-pound bag of rice. So we are not going to starve. What a reality check, when you do that as opposed to trotting down to Coles for a few things before the kids get home from school.

I'm back to making the yeast mess again, too. Oh, joy!

14th August 2010

Hi everyone!

This is the email I have been dying to write for 4 and a half months now. The boat is now officially … (here's the f word) … FINISHED!!

She is still on the beach … BUT … her hulls are stronger than they have ever been. She is fared. She is antifouled (although Andrew is very unhappy with the finish, due to the product we used that's not really designed for this, even tho we were told it was!) … and she looks like any yacht waiting in a yard to be put in the water.

We rigged her yesterday, as the locals thought our main halyard looked better in smaller pieces on the front of their boats. We tried to get one from Guam but that just didn't happen, but we rigged something up that will get us to Palau.

Today we work on the 'L' word. So keep your fingers crossed for us, as we lower the boat onto tracks and put a frame under her, with eight empty fuel drums in a stocks type structure, and then hopefully slide her into the water on low tide and float her off as the tide rises. Very weather dependent, so may take a day or so.

So hopefully the next instalment will be the L word email.

Thanks so much for all your support, and emails. Palau here we come!

Cheers from

Jen and the crew moving back into the blue

Here are snippets from some of the 50ish responses we received to that email.

Hello,

Great news, congratulations! We still find it so hard to imagine being on Mogmog for such a long time! Great to see what strength, determination and distilled water can do!

I hope the raft works well with the tides.

We are now in Bali, Richard, Cathy, Annie and Oli will be joining us and sailing to Komodo next week. We set sail for West Aus in October, then to Sydney for December to start the race to Hobart.

Safe sailing to Palau, sure you will have a great welcoming party!

Regards Gina and the crew on Titania.

Titania of Cowes

* * *

Hello Barries,

thankyou so much for your group email ... I think of you all daily ... and hadnt heard back from you, was getting worried!

well, you have well and truly stood the biggest test of time ... and finally palau is in site!

wishing you all the best of luck with the launch ... lady windy will be sooooo happy to get her belly wet ...

big loves to the littlins, you must be so proud of them, tell you what ... i dont recon they will ever complain about being bored, or hungry ever again!!

Freddy ... you are an absolute legend ... i knew you could do it ... if anyone can, it's you!

and my gorgie jen, well, you are just the glue really ... what a strong woman you are, im so proud to have you as my friend.

so keep strong, smiles on faces, and think of the wine and ice cold beer that awaits you ... your mates in Palau must be counting down ... miss you all so much ...

love always,

lou, and Gus and his dad ...

* * *

Yippie I aye mee harty

Don't forget to attach a rope to the plug in the middle of the island?

As you sail off into the blue 'pull hard' and before your eyes it will sink gently below the sea. (ok just dreaming)

Good luck

Regards

Bruce Strapp

* * *

We were just thinking about you yesterday and wondering of your progress.

What a wonderful thing, to be going back in the water!! Soon you will be back to civilization with food, clothes, supplies, laundry service, a restaurant and cool refreshing beer! We are truly impressed with your herculean effort. And Palau … not a better place to regroup.

Congratulations.

Amy and Bill

THIRTY-FOUR

IS THIS BOAT EVER GONNA MOVE?

CLANG CLANG CLANG
  CLANG CLANG CLANG
  CLANG CLANG CLANG
  CLANG CLANG CLANG CLANG CLANG CLANG
CLANG CLANG CLANG
  CLANG.

Time to rise and shine. It's Sunday, anniversary of the finishing of the church and also the anniversary of the end of World War II. A big Mass is planned for this morning, followed by a feast in celebration. Juanito has made a point of asking us not to bring a thing. We have done enough.

What's really busting our chops is that we have to start lowering the boat down off its supports today! Currently, the front of it is held up from the ground by mini keels — sometimes known as sacrificial keels — which are attached to the hulls for beaching the boat. The mini keels are both sitting on stacks of timber 40mm thick and 7 deep, so nearly 30cm high. Doesn't sound like a lot, does it? At the back, *Windie* is supported by the original frame that took out Glen's hand. It has a pillar at either side, approximately 1.8 metres high. These two pillars are also made of 40mm deep planks. Where we didn't have 40mm to use, it was two lots of 20.

Andrew has constructed the track, or series of skids, which we will run out on the fly as we take the boat from the beach down to the water. Our immediate task is to painstakingly lower the boat onto the track. We need the boat to sit 100mm from the ground so we can slide a skid in under the keels. Our plan is to use our World War II screw jack to lift the boat, working one weight-bearing point at a time and slipping out one piece of timber at a time. In other words, we'll go to the first corner, raise it, remove one board then lower the corner again. Then we'll move to the next corner and do the same thing, and so on. A very long, slow process. Mind you, the boat weighs 8000 kilograms when it's empty, so it's probably double that now that the girls have moved in all our worldly possessions.

If ever we have needed focus, it's now. Andrew is a mess. His eyes are bugging out of his head and bright, bright green — never a good sign. His veins are prominent. It's abundantly clear to me that the automatic pilot part of his head is kicking in. Thank God his automatic pilot is a good one!

We began on the starboard bow. As Andrew wound up the jack, it began to look precarious. The angle was wrong.

'Shit, it's stuffed! It's going to go!'

Oh, shit! We scrambled around gathering planks to put forward of the jack, in the hope we could make a pillar before the jack failed completely. Just as we got to the last 10mm, the jack sheared on its screw and the boat fell onto the pillar we had made. I jumped through the nonexistent roof!

Even though *Windrider* had landed on the pillar, she'd sustained damage. Andrew was beside himself. I looked at the damage. Not sooooo bad. It will need to be patched up and glassed, though. As for the jack, who knows?

It's 8.30 now. Time for Mass. Despite the gravity of our situation, I need to get there, even if Andrew doesn't. With pictures in my head of smashed boats and crushed husbands, I go to church, jumping at every noise. I register the sound of the grinder. That means Andrew is repairing the jack. That has to be okay. Finally, after more than two hours, Mass is over, and I race back to him with the girls.

My husband's face is pure stress. He has a jack plate in place in the aft starboard hull. He has retrieved the snapped bit of screw and there is enough screw left to be able to continue using the jack. He looks me straight in the eye. 'I don't know we can do this.'

'Come on. Let's just do it and see how we go.'

'I don't know, Jen. I don't know if I can.'

'Let's eat this elephant one bite at a time.'

Over the next several hours we made excruciatingly slow progress as we moved from corner to corner, repositioned the jack, changed the angle of the jack and took out 40mm of wood here, 20mm there. Andrew's stress level did not alter from beginning to end. By 4pm, he was utterly drained, emotionally and physically. He'd wound the jack up and down perhaps 50 times, taking the weight of the boat onto the jack and off again. All up, we had lowered the boat halfway. So much for leaving today! No chance.

Juanito came by for a drink and a chat. We had a good laugh, which had a great effect on Andrew. At that, we chucked it in for the day and sat down to some feast food.

Each family had been given food to take home and eat. Juanito had made sure we received heaps of food, which is wonderful of him.

After Juanito had made his goodbyes and the kids had gone to bed, Andrew and I sat up the front of the boat in the wind and darkness, just the two of us. We shared a beer and talked about tomorrow.

Will this plan actually work? How far would we get? In a couple of days from now, will the last five months be stretching on and on or will we realise this dream and sail out of here?

* * *

Mike arrived bright and early next morning. Most people here, you just wouldn't want helping, but Mike is resourceful, clever —

quick in mind and on his feet — and strong. His input is always thought out carefully, and invariably useful.

Again we attacked it one bit at a time. It was a lot like playing that game called Jenga, where you take a wooden block from a tower and transfer it to the top of the tower: the object is to make the tallest tower you can. The back had to come down 30cm, the front 8cm. That just felt wrong. But 40mm by 40mm we took out the back, and then took a plank from the front on each side. By lunchtime, the boat Jenga was complete. *Windrider* was down and resting on the skids Andrew had built.

These skids consist of a single plank resting on a slightly larger plank with sides, and plenty of grease between the two planks. The idea is that the boat slides down on its skids and then we put more skids in front of it. This way we build a track all the way down to the water.

Lunch was a modest affair, and was only there due to Juanito's kindness. We're now out of all meat, fruit and vegies, so our diet will consist of noodles and rice; when this is gone, that's it.

And if that's not bad enough, we're reduced to drinking woobla again. Ripper. Love that yeast drink ... *not*!

* * *

Literally out of the blue, Amos appeared! That was a brilliant surprise because the whole time we've been here, he's never been to Mogmog. He explained that he had a sightseeing charter and decided to bring his clients to Mogmog — so he could visit us and see our progress. A real live visitor! There were big hugs all round. We showed him all we have done, but he could only stay for a little while. After a quick cuppa, he was off, but it was great to be able to say farewell to him in person.

Our next job was to attach the temporary frame to the boat. It consists of two brackets that go across the boat underneath. These house two rows of four fuel drums each. These are braced to the sides, and the whole lot is attached to a triangular timber structure that extends from the back of the frame to an apex 60cm in front of the forward bracket, similar to a boat trailer frame.

It had taken two days to make this erection, as Andrew calls it. He is still in a bad state and now not sleeping either, in spite of some Vicodan we found left from other yachties. Yeah, I know this is not quite best practice, but hey, this is one of those times when you gotta do what you gotta do.

Finally, it's time to see if this bastard will budge. We moved the block and tackle from the front, where it has been attached to a palm tree for months, and attached it to an anchor that Mike set out on the reef.

By now the peanut gallery were all in place, including Edward, Persley's dad, who has taken it upon himself to give a hand. Yikes! This is a guy who set fire to great chunks of the island when he last helped with a burn-off! There is a fair bit of genetics in Persley's condition. I realise Edward is helping only because he has seen me hand out yeast drink to the helpers at the end of the day. It wouldn't worry me, except it's bloody dangerous. At any time, the boat could run away or the chain block snap. You need to be alert and fast to react, and Edward ain't either of those!

So with peanut gallery ensconced and workers stressed, we pulled … and pulled … and pulled … And nothing. Not a bloody thing.

THIRTY-FIVE

EXERCISING MORE PATIENCE

Andrew gazed at the boat that would not budge, the look on his face one of utter devastation.

There was nothing else for it: out came the yeast drink, and we sat down with Edward (ripper!), Mike and Juanito to think and bat around ideas. About an hour and a half later, we'd come up with four plans and variations on each of them. The thing about these guys is that they are used to solving problems with absolutely no resources, so their ideas are practical, simple and doable.

Juanito's idea was to insert metal tubing between the two planks. Andrew thought that slipping some 20mm wood as a halfway house between the two layers could work. Mike suggested jamming a steel lintel between the planks.

Thanking our brains trust, we packed it in for the day. A thoroughly dejected Andrew shovelled food in his face, took a

Vicodan and then hit the hay. An hour or so later he woke feeling hot, uncomfortable, and with an upset stomach. Yearning for breeze, he went and lay down on the trampolines on the front. A little while later I joined him, as did Moggsie. We shared a fitful night's sleep until it rained on us at 4am. It was a shock, at that hour, to find a man standing in the darkness, just standing and watching us. Very unnerving.

In the morning we rose groggily and managed to organise coffee. According to the tide report we looked up on the HF, even if we had managed to splash *Windie*, the tide wouldn't have been right anyway. It would be Saturday before the tide was optimal — two days away — and this coincided with a full moon at night, which would make for fantastic sailing.

Coincidentally, the supply ship will also be here on Saturday, so I had a 'swallow the pride' moment and picked up the phone to place another order with Ali, hoping he'd be okay with this, given the amount we owe them. Phew! Luck was on my side.

After weighing up our options, Andrew and I decided to hunt for metal tubing to give Juanito's idea a go. On our travels, we dropped into Raymond's house to ask if he knew where any tubing might be. On the table lay a book that looked remarkably like a SIDE workbook Shan uses for school. Knowing I was being very rude, I casually ambled over and picked it up. Guess what? It's the set we have been waiting for for months! Deb said she sent it maybe eight weeks ago. What I'd spotted turned out to be part of one book. Amos had told us that a few weeks ago he had dropped off two boxes for us in Falalop. It appeared that someone must have collected our mail from Falalop, opened the two boxes addressed to us and stolen the contents. It's moments like this that undo so much.

Naturally, Raymond and his family knew nothing about it. Right now, though, we have more pressing matters to attend to!

* * *

Having found what we were after, Andrew and I went back to the boat and cut the tubing into 8-inch lengths. Mike was there again. Next we jacked and wedged up the board off the skids and shoved the steel in between the two layers.

Once this was done, we loosened the various restraints at the front of the boat and tightened the chain block at the back and … *Windrider* moved! I think we all screamed! I certainly did. The boat slid happily for about 15cm and then stopped as the front rope tautened. Wow! It's going to work.

The change in Andrew was instant! This morning he was ready to chuck it all in, and now he has a grin from ear to ear. I raced up to Juanito's place to tell him he was a genius!

If this 16,000 kilograms of boat can move 15cm, it can get to the water.

So Saturday is L-day; I can't say the word or I'll jinx it. The plan is that we go to the water and receive our delivery from the ship. With our track record, you just watch — it'll be a bloody typhoon. Keep you posted.

After lunch, Andrew and I went for a wander to try and

track down the schoolwork. The names Wyno and Lorna had appeared all through the workbook we found, so we started by asking them. They are the children of Arthur, the 'doctor'. They were very defensive. Very, very defensive. Naturally, they knew nothing of it, but they had got the workbook from Kirra. It so happens that Kirra is three years old. Ripper.

Nonetheless, determined to follow it up, we went to see the child's mother and Sarah, who was with Kirra at the women's house at the time we figure the mail should have arrived. Before long, a crowd of women surrounded us. Sarah predictably said 'I don't know' to every question asked. We tried to make a joke of the 'I don't knows', saying it was the only response we ever get to any question we ask, and we dared them to answer a question, any question with something other than 'I don't know'. Not one of them could.

Utterly exasperated, we left; it was going nowhere. It's a violation of basic decency, to my mind, that even children should have no compunction about stealing mail addressed to others. At the slightest hint of being asked to account for this behaviour, the people signal that they don't care and close ranks.

Putting aside those principles for a minute, I think it amounts to theft, too, as there are about $250 worth of resources in the packs Deb sends us. There are library books, DVDs, art supplies and so on — all expensive. Who pays for them? It really takes the shine off. Mind you, the shine was pretty scuffed anyway.

I wandered up to talk with Glen about it because he drives the boat to Falalop and collects the mail. Guess what? He didn't know anything about it. But he did point out that two or three weeks ago the island had no fuel, so he didn't go. Only Arthur could go, as he had fuel. Guess what again? Arthur is the father of Wyno and Lorna. Here we are, back to the beginning once more.

I give up. Had enough of going around in circles. I'll seek my happiness in my own camp, with my own family and boat. As for the locals, with the exception of Mike and Juanito, I'll put them out of my mind.

* * *

At 8.30 that night, Mike arrived agitated and upset. Tuba-fuelled, he stormed up onto the boat and said he wanted to talk to us *now*!

'Okay, fine. What is it?'

'You are telling people I stole your betel nut that you bought in Yap.'

'Mike, we never said that, and we never thought that.'

'Who do you think stole it?'

'I have no idea!'

'Mike, we said to you yesterday that you are our friend.'

'That means nothing!'

'Why do you say that?'

'Because anyone on this island who says that to someone means that it is for that day, and never any more than that.'

'Mike, where we come from, if we say you are a friend, it means you are a friend forever. And a friend would never say that you stole from us.'

'Really? Man, I have to get off this fucking island. I'm stuck here for the rest of my life, and I can't get off.' Tears ran freely down his face.

'Mike, maybe we can change that. Maybe we can get you to Australia, and you can stay with us and look at maybe getting a job.'

'Do you really mean that?'

'Are you our friend?'

'Yes.'

* * *

A rough, grey dawn breaks. It's Saturday; it's supposed to be *the* day that all the blood, sweat and tears of the last five months come together.

As I watched the swell rolling in, I tensed. Andrew's mood exactly matched the weather. He was grumpy from the moment he woke. I just shut up.

By 6.30am he had made up his mind that trying to get *Windrider* afloat today wouldn't work. Mike didn't appear until 10.30 because he had come to the same conclusion. As had Juanito.

The weather settled excruciatingly slowly. Andrew's mood did not.

The supply ship arrived, and Andrew said we should both go out with the dinghy to retrieve our stuff. Guess who was there? Aiden, Juanito's son, and my rescuer the day in Yap when the boat left without me! Standing in the hold, yelling, 'Jen! Jen! Your stuff is all there,' as he pointed among the tons of belatedly arriving food, belongings and hardware items for all the outer islands.

'Thanks! You're a legend. *Again!*'

A huge grin was the answer I received, then the men organised a chain, and the multitudinous piles started to move rapidly off the supply ship.

As we arranged, I followed the first of our boxes. Just as I scrambled up through the hatch of the supply ship, the box disappeared in front of my eyes, over the top of the deck. Who cares; it was only chicken noodles. I watched the rest arrive, including VB beer! Ali, you're a bloody legend! I dived onto the dinghy after our gear, and we were off. Andrew stayed to help the men, and I signalled to the girls on the beach that I had our gear and was coming in. They met me with a wheelbarrow, and two or three men came to help. Among them was Rio, who I had last talked to in relation to the girls' wrecked bikes, and I had forbidden him to come near us or our belongings again. I gave him a grin and a thanks. His smile lit his face.

I'm finding this hard to write. Everything's becoming too close to the wire. So much of what I'm trying to describe is too close to the heart, and the emotions are becoming difficult to both define and control.

Diana, Shan and I had all our order stowed away on the boat by the time Andrew reappeared, and the beer was all but cold. Ali, in his now infinite helpfulness, had given up on the freezer on the ship and decided we deserved better than foam cooler boxes, and had been providing us with Esky coolers at $50 a pop! We had just taken delivery of the fourth; we already had two when we first arrived.

Suddenly I hear, 'Jen ... Jen!' and there is Mike, racing down the beach towards us carrying a box of noodles! Gotta love him! As he came up onto the deck, puffing hard, I said to him, 'Swap you the box of noodles for an Esky and a bottle of Bacardi!'

The grin was worth a million.

Later that night, Mike reappeared and asked to come on board. There was something he wanted to tell us. It was that not one person on the island had believed that we could succeed. In fact, he said, they had been just waiting for us to fail, to give up and finally leave the boat to them — as they felt it should have been all the way along. He said that he was there because he believed we could do it, and as he was our friend, he wanted to be part of it with us. I think there were a fair few tears right about then.

THIRTY-SIX

TIME AND TIDE DON'T WAIT

Sunday dawned almost stubbornly. We had been waiting for it for hours. Andrew dawned equally stubbornly. His demeanour became more and more determined and stubborn over the course of the dawn until he was downright scary. He asked my opinion. When I gave it, I got a 'No way!' response. It had to be his way.

Unbidden, Mike arrived. Church was forgotten.

At about 7am, Andrew said quietly, 'This is it; it's today. Are you ready?'

Shit, shit, shit, shit, shit! My heart was pounding; I sucked in air and nodded.

The plan was to follow the tide down. Somehow, the tubing — Juanito's inspiration — had partially impregnated itself into the planking of our skids, stopping any movement. While the boys busied themselves at the back of the boat, fixing that up,

I took up my position at the front of the boat, pulling taut the anchor line around a tree and back to the windlass. Mike took an anchor about 50 metres beyond the reef and attached it there, and then they attached the smaller block and tackle around the apex frame, and the larger block and tackle from the loop of the smaller one and out to the anchor chain.

It took about 20 agonising minutes before the boat moved. Progress was only 5ish centimetres; this time there were no accompanying screams of excitement. Even the kids were silent as scared determination took over us all. Reading that back, it sounds melodramatic, yet that's the level of emotion that pervaded. There were only the three of us doing this, and we were committed with every fibre of our being, and yes, we were scared. If we didn't get this boat off now, then we would wait a month for the tide to be right again. By then, the boat would most likely be smashed on the reef, and our frayed minds just couldn't bend around that thought.

It took the three of us until 2pm to inch *Windie* down to the reef. Each time she moved — always jerkily — I made a mental tick. That was one more move forward (albeit in a backwards direction) that we no longer had to make.

The tide began returning a little too early for our speed. Then, when we were 2 feet short of where we needed to be, the frame apex pulled out and away from the frame itself. The sound was sickening. Had we failed here? In this, the worst possible spot?

Totally committed, we had nowhere else to go. At that point there was no alternative but to wait for the tide. I was shattered.

The next thing I knew, I was waking up, unaware that I had dropped off to sleep until that moment. In the middle of everything, I had just shut down; I must have gone out like a light. What roused me was the sound of two Yanmar 30s revving their guts out in reverse.

Juanito was there and had been for ages, unknown to me. It was now 6pm.

The tide was going to be leaving at seven. We weren't quite there.

Mike was on the block and tackle, now wrapped around what was left of the frame with the diesel drums. The structure itself was holding.

Andrew was at the throttles. A crowd — curious — had begun to gather.

I jumped off the boat to ascertain our depth; with just 10 minutes of tide to go, we still weren't there.

Catherine, the Peace Corps teacher from New Mexico, spotted me, raced up and gave me a huge hug. 'You can *do this*,' she literally screamed.

'I don't know, Cath. If we don't do it in 10 minutes, it can't be done.'

'Then get back fucking well up there and *do it*!'

I never saw her again.

At two minutes past seven, the revving Yanmars managed to get the boat to move nearly nowhere.

But then, as if from another nowhere, the locals came and started to push. Once again, it was the villagers versus the boat.

As every wave came through, Andrew would rev the guts out of the engines, and Mike would wind that block and tackle. And the locals would scream a war cry and push.

And agonising inch by slow-motion agonising inch, *Windie* came free.

At the exact moment she did — stuffed if I know how he could even think of this, let alone do it — this is what I hear at about a zillion decibels:

bom bom da da dom
bom bom da da dom
bom bom da da da da da da
bom bom da da da da da da
bom bom da da da di da da
bom bom da da da di da da
Pretty woman walking down the street.

What do you do with a boy like that?

As *Windie* continued her slow, majestic passage over the reef, Mike and about six men walked with her. There was never more than an inch of water under her as we walked her that 50 metres. Then she slid over the edge of the reef and stopped at anchor, exactly as intended.

I have to confess that the rest of that night was a bit of a blur.

* * *

It took until Tuesday to get the frame out from underneath *Windie*. Not because it was a big job. It was just that we were too emotionally undone.

On Monday, we saw Juanito and said our goodbyes. We promised him he would hear from us, and he will.

Although we hadn't asked for help, on Tuesday morning, up popped Mike and Aiden who had swum out. Between us, we removed the frame and swam it ashore.

Later, Andrew, the girls and I wandered through the village saying our parting words to the islanders, and dropping in to a few houses: Raymond's, for instance. There were a few things we especially wanted to give to certain people: an Esky to Ludis, the lovely lime lady; a bed to Mike's daughter, Raelene.

After one last 'see ya' to Juanito, it was time to go. A handful of individuals followed us back to the beach. There were six: Juanito; Raymond; Mike and his wife; Aiden and his son, Dylan. Just them out of 200.

Out of the blue, Mike left and then came screaming back along the sand, holding not one but two woven baskets handmade by his wife, Marylou, which he presented to Andrew as a gesture of friendship.

As our dinghy headed to the waiting boat for the last time, Moggie's brothers, Colonel and Arbi, swam out as a guard of honour … so we had to turn around and take them back.

Goodbye, Mogmog. And this time, it really is goodbye. Diana and Shannon went up on the bow with Moggie, who had adjusted immediately to being a 'cat–dog'. While she scampered all over, the girls put their feet over the front and watched Mogmog disappear. Andrew and I set the sails and then looked back. We were about a mile off by now. We sat together, and turned to the view in front, and couldn't say a word.

* * *

Our trip back to Palau was uneventful. Wind was in short supply, so we motored most of the way, arriving in Palau on Friday morning. At 4am we rose to the sight of the hills of Babeldaub, the largest island in the archipelago. More tears.

We cleared customs and quarantine and had Moggie vaccinated. Then we sailed straight over to Sam's.

Our friends had heard we were coming, so for their entertainment, we did a lap around the area in front of the bar with — you guessed it — 'Pretty Woman' blaring out.

Before we'd even managed to pick up the mooring, Dennis and Carol were flying out in their dinghy, brandishing a glass of wine and a beer. Gotta love them!

Everyone was waiting for us at the bar. The mood was phenomenal — euphoric and totally intoxicating. I think it'll take a week to recover from Sam's hug. People were crowding around to bestow hugs, drinks and congratulations. Carol came up with a huge basket of fruit. Diana flew up, holding in her hand an invitation to a party for the next day. Dermott, the party father, came up.

'Dermott, we haven't been here 20 minutes and you've got an invitation for the girls.'

'Well, it's been written for two weeks!'

'I can't organise a present that fast.'

'I don't want a present, I want your kids.'

'Well, you *can* have them.'

'Great.'

Then he disappeared, only to reappear immediately brandishing another bottle of wine.

Not every face was familiar. Among the people we met were Brian and Mary-Alice, fantastic people who had sent us food from Yap, as they are friends with the owners of Pacific Missionary Aviation, and had heard of our situation. In the course of the conversation Brian said he was a pilot. I mentioned I have a licence, and he asked what I fly, and then I asked him what he flies.

'F16s.'

I felt like an abject idiot.

We spent a fantastic time, drank too much and watched the sun set on both the day and the adventure.

Next morning, I woke with a jolt at 5am and experienced a huge surge of excitement. I climbed out of the hatch and snuck up on deck. Moggie joined me, and I sat —otherwise alone — while the sun crept all too fast up the beautiful green rock islands around me. The water was still and deep, deep green.

I really don't know that there is a more beautiful place in the world.

EPILOGUE

Today is 2nd April 2011, a year and a weekish since our unceremonious dumping on Mogmog. This day finds us anchored off the town of Puerto Princessa, on the eastern coast of the westernmost island of the Philippines. It's a great spot, with a bustling town and fantastic scenery.

After leaving Mogmog, we spent five months in Palau. Almost every bit of *Windrider* that hadn't broken down on us on Mogmog has since done so because of salt and water immersion. This meant that we spent ages waiting for parts — and for the next thing to break down. Mind you, Palau is a terrific place to be stuck.

Mogmog has stayed on our minds and has continued to inspire conflicting feelings in me. From Palau we sent all kinds of packages to people there, including a TV and DVD player for

Mike; school supplies and a backpack for Raymond's daughter; a pocketknife for Jarrod; chocolate for Ellie; cigarettes and vodka for Juanito; and a huge box of general, day-to-day stuff like lighters and rice. Our publishers, HarperCollins, posted stuff too. Even though everyone had our Palau address, no one bothered to contact us; not one word of thanks or a hello has reached us. Sharlet, Aiden's wife, arrived in Palau to do some study, so we took her out to lunch and asked her how everyone was. At the end of the lunch, she asked for a loan to tide her over. She would pay us back in two weeks, she said. Well, it's been a long two weeks, and we have had no info from her about the island.

Over the last six months, we have spoken to many people who have travelled extensively through the islands, and have compared notes about this 'gimme' mind-set. The very definite consensus is that the local people didn't always expect handouts, and that it came about after the Americans started splashing around resources and money during World War II, because of the strategic importance of these islands. After decades of continued funding, there has developed a pervading expectation among the islanders that they need only to ask to receive, and they become quite perplexed when what they ask for is not forthcoming. The idea of going out and working for what they require has become entirely alien to them.

Somehow, that attitude doesn't appear to have taken root in the Philippines. Where we are, the people work so hard, all day, every day. In conversation, whenever I have bounced around with the locals the idea that they could be receiving handouts, they are flummoxed. If you want something you work for it. One girl looked at me in amazement and said, 'But if I don't work, I will be poor.' What a different mentality.

I have come to the sad realisation that there is nothing much we can do to genuinely help the people of Mogmog. Whatever we do, they will expect more of the same, and they will do nothing to help themselves. Juanito wanted water catchments. I spoke to AusAID, the Australian Government's overseas aid agency, and they were very definite that the people who require whatever it is must apply themselves, not someone else on their behalf. I now understand why.

Our daughters have emerged from their Mogmog experience remarkably unscathed. They slotted back into Palauan life like greasy pigs — quickly teamed up again with Sam's, Dermott's and Jay's kids, and relearned what real friendships are all about. They had a ball. Dermott's daughter is coming to stay with us in Perth for a three-month exchange-type trip, and Sam is bringing his family to Perth at the end of the year.

Leaving Palau for the second time was way easier than the first. The first time it felt like goodbye to some great people we were going to miss and maybe never see again. The second time, the roots are much deeper, and Palau has become a second home to us. These are friends for life now, so this time it was 'See ya', not 'Goodbye'.

Moggie is safely in quarantine in Sydney. Tight quarantine restrictions meant she couldn't come through the Philippine islands and Indonesia with us. Some wonderful friends did all the paperwork and vet stuff and got her on the plane to Oz, where she is halfway through her gaol sentence. When she escapes, she flies back to Perth to stay with friends until we get home. Miss that bundle of fluff with clattery claws. We call her the little brown dog with the great big heart.

For Andrew and me, the world has become before — 'BMM' — and after — 'AMM'. I really don't want that middle bit, the 'on Mogmog' chapter of our lives, to be so defining. Psychologically, it has taken its toll on us: the old confidence has taken a battering. We sail differently now. We tend to be a bit more defensive all round, and I don't just mean the technical aspects of sailing. I even wonder whether some post-traumatic stress has crept into the picture. Does that sound melodramatic? Possibly. Anyway, I am hoping that time will heal, as it usually does.

And from here?

We are heading to Borneo this week and will meet up with family in Kota Kinabalu. From there, it's around Borneo, down to Bali, and back onto Australian shores in Broome. So we are on the homeward leg of this particular voyage. We need to get home for the girls, so that they can go to high school with their friends. Long ago, we said that it wouldn't work sailing with teenagers because they are not going to want to know us then. Andrew and I have been very fortunate to have had this time with them at the age that they are. I reckon they will grow up and buy farms!

EPILOGUE

As for the future — are we over this? Perhaps it's too early to tell, but Andrew and I occasionally find ourselves talking about destinations, changes to the boat, or even a newer boat, so I don't think this experience has knocked the stuffing out of us yet.

ACKNOWLEDGMENTS

Our experiences over the five months and two days that we were on Mogmog showed us what friendship really means. The following people made it possible to succeed at what seemed to be impossible. It must be said that support came on two levels. There was physical, practical help, which was given generously by many, and there was also — and perhaps just as importantly — personal and moral support, the gratitude for which … well, words just don't do it justice.

If I've missed you, come and tell me, and I'll make it up to you.

To Diana and Shannon Barrie — what troopers these kids are.

Thanks to our mums, Maureen Gregory and Dawn Barrie, for unfailing support on so many levels.

To my dad, Peter Griffiths, and wicked stepmum, Valli, for practical help, packages and friendship.

To our sisters, Melinda Fitzgerald and Suzzanne Laidlaw, banker and PA extraordinaire, and chief moral and chocolate support.

Our great mates, Paul Walker and Fiona Sarre, who managed to find everything we needed, everywhere in the world, and then get it to us, right down to hundreds of DVDs that are now somewhere on Mogmog. Thank you so much.

The Staines family, who have very kindly given Moggie a second home until we get back.

The Barton, Poh and Strapp families, all of North Perth, who gave the kids, and their parents, their friends back home by constant email.

Paul and Vanessa Montague, for freight and friendship.

Lou Belleville, Scott Shepherd and Brendan Sayers, for care packages, practicalities and, again, friendship.

Louise Inglis, for emails that saved the sanity, and Nikki Turner, for writing an email every single day of the last month because I needed it.

Debra Reynolds, the girls' wonderful teacher and now friend, who provided the only stability in the whole thing. Thanks, Deb.

Ian 'Macca' and Lee Kelly of 'Australia All Over' — a friendly voice and a slice of Aus.

Bones Menkens, for all things Brizzie and Bunnings.

Jeff Frazer of Yanmar Australia.

Reg and Helen of Pacific Flier.

Les of CT Freight.

Anthony of ATL Composites

And in Palau:

Sam Scott, a great mate, for whom nothing is too much trouble.

Dennis and Carol Whalen, Mr Logistics and Mr Fixit, and two wonderful friends to boot.

Jason Hopcus, weatherman extraordinaire and, again, a great friend.

Dermott Keane, friend and Mr Everything at Sam's.

Yvonne Otero, who did all the paperwork to get past quarantine for Moggie after we had to leave her there due to visa expiry.

Monica Minciu, vet on Palau, who did way more paperwork than you would believe, at no cost, to help us with Moggie.

And in Yap:

Bill Acker, a good and generous man.

Amos, the PMA pilot, who allowed us to use his place as a delivery point, who managed our 'bank' on Mogmog, and who did myriad things way above and beyond what could be asked for. I don't think it could've worked without you, Amos. Thank you.

Richard and Cathy Dobbs, and Gina, captain of *Titania*, without whom this book would not have happened.

Dominic and Ali of the Yap store — you were great.

And on Mogmog:

Juanito and Ellie, who allowed us to realise our hopes, and who gave us a place to stay and also allowed us to be part of the community for five months. Leaving all disputes behind, I will always be hugely grateful to you, and fond of you.

Mike Taueg, who was there and believed to the end.

Raymond, for solutions, laughs and friendship.

Alberta, for bananas, advice and companionship.

Ludis, the lovely lime lady, for limes, advice and an even keel.

Mario, for security on the ships.

Catherine, the Peace Corps worker, for honesty even when it hurt.

Janet Whittaker of the Australian Embassy, Pohnpei, who provided security and patrol ship diversions.

And at Harper Collins:

Jeanne Ryckmans and Anne Reilly, who thought this might work and then proceeded to achieve that goal at great distances, with little to no communications.

And, finally:

To Andrew — thank you for everything.